AN ANGEL

Of

LIGHT

False Prophets and Deceiving Spirits at Work Today in the Church and World

Eddie L. Hyatt

HYATT PRESS * 2016

Publish, and set up a standard; publish and conceal not (Jeremiah 50:2)

ANGELS OF LIGHT
By Eddie L. Hyatt
© 2018 by Hyatt International Ministries, Incorporated
ALL RIGHTS RESERVED.

Published by Hyatt Press
A Subsidiary of Hyatt Int'l Ministries, Incorporated

Mailing Address:
P. O. Box 3877
Grapevine, TX 76099-3877

Internet Addresses:
Email: dreddiehyatt@gmail.com
Web Site: www.eddiehyatt.com
Social Media: Eddie L. Hyatt

Unless otherwise indicated, all Scripture quotations
are taken from the New Kings James Version of the Bible. ©
1979, 1980, 1982 by Thomas Nelson, Inc. Publishers.

ISBN: 978-1-888435-25-2

Printed in the United States of America

Foreword

I wish I had written this book. It is so needed in our day. Lest you think we are critical, make no mistake about it! Eddie and I love the activity of the Holy Spirit. Over many decades, we have observed and participated in various trends among us. We have rejoiced in the real, but we have grieved when Believers have embraced the counterfeit.

This book will help distinguish between what is really of God and what not. And it will embolden us to answer two questions vital in keeping us safe in spiritual things.

First, when Scripture does not endorse a teaching, practice, manifestation, or experience, can I accept what Scripture says and align with God's Word and Character?

Second, do I recognize the values that are driving me to pursue certain spiritual experiences? For example, does my natural human need to feel significant provoke me to pursue what I think makes me look important or feel good?

The facts from Scripture and Church history in this book will witness with the Holy Spirit in us and remind us what it really means to be a Christian. We'll be renewed in our calling to know Him and in our commission to make Him known. And we'll more accurately fulfil this passage: *As He is, so are we in this world (1 John 4:17, NKJV). O people, the LORD has told you what is good, and this is what he requires of you: to do what is right, to love mercy, and to walk humbly with your God (Micah 6:8: New Living Translation).*

So then, may God use this book to point us once again to Jesus and help us recognize and cooperate with His Spirit.

Susan Stubbs Hyatt, D.Min., M.A., M.A, Cert. Life Coach, Lic. Teacher
Grapevine, Texas. August 10, 2018

3

Table of Contents

Preface

In my book, *2000 Years of Charismatic Christianity*, I documented the dynamic, miraculous work of the Holy Spirit from the Day of Pentecost to the present time. I also documented the intensifying of the Holy Spirit's work since the turn of the twentieth century, with virtually all denominations now open to the miraculous gifts of the Spirit, and the formation of thousands of new Pentecostal and charismatic churches and denominations.

Even as I was doing the research for that book, however, I was being made aware of the demonic deceptions that arose in virtually every revival. Thomas Coke, John Wesley's colleague and biographer, wrote of how Satan sought to destroy the great eighteenth century Methodist revival with counterfeit gifts and manifestations. He also acknowledged that it was not something new.

Those who have read the accounts of the great revivals of true religion in many parts of Europe, and in our own country in particular, will easily perceive the sameness of those devices of Satan whereby he perverts the right ways of the Lord.

The devices Satan uses again and again in revival are spiritual pride and a neglect of Scripture for the pursuit of esoteric, spiritual experiences. Coke mentions this in his biography, saying that Wesley was called upon to oppose several great deceptions that arose in the revival. According to Coke, one of the deceptions was,

Attention to dreams, visions, and men's own imaginations and feelings, without bringing them to the only sure test, the oracles of God.[1]

I am a life-long, committed Pentecostal-Charismatic who values the miraculous and dynamic work of the Holy Spirit My earliest memories include being in church meetings where gifts of the Holy Spirit were being manifest and prayer for the sick was being offered. I remember as a child going with my family to great healing revivals under the giant tents of Oral Roberts and William Freeman.

I lived through the great healing revivals of the 1950s, the great Charismatic Renewal of the 1970s (when I was supernaturally called into the ministry), the Word of Faith revival of the 1980s, the Toronto and Pensacola revivals of the 1990s and the work of the Holy Spirit since that time.

Yes, I value the work of the Holy Spirit, but I have learned from experience that all that glitters is not gold and that Christians, perhaps as never before, need to listen to the words of Paul who, in II Corinthians 11:13-15, warned,

> *For such are false apostles, deceitful workers, transforming themselves into apostles of Christ. And no wonder! For Satan himself transforms himself into an angel of light. Therefore it is no great thing if his ministers also transform themselves into ministers of righteousness.*

---

[1] Dr. Coke and Mr. Moore, *Life of the Rev. John Wesley, A.M.* (Philadelphia: Printed by Parry Hall, MDCCXCII), 157.

The purpose of this book is not to be critical. The purpose of this book is to help this generation realize that along with the promised outpouring of the Holy Spirit in the last days, there are many Scriptural warnings of wide-spread deception that will also characterize the end times. I see signs everywhere of this deception, especially in the modern charismatic movement.

It behooves us, therefore, to be equipped to discern the true from the false, the real from the fake. As John the Apostle exhorted in I John 4:1,

Beloved, do not believe every spirit, but test the spirits whether they are of God, because many false prophets have gone out into the world.

Chapter I

The Warnings
of Jesus and Scripture

For false christs and false prophets will arise and show great signs and wonders to deceive, if possible, even the elect.

Matthew 24:24

Take heed that no one deceives you, were the first words from the mouth of Jesus in response to a question from His disciples concerning the "sign" of His coming and the end of the age (Matthew 24:4). Their question was prompted when Jesus stunned them with a prediction concerning the destruction of the temple in Jerusalem.

It happened when the disciples were admiring the Jerusalem temple with its massive stones and ornate architecture. When they called Jesus' attention to its magnificence, He astonished them by saying, *Assuredly, I say to you, not one stone shall be left here upon another, that shall not be thrown down.* (Matthew 24:2).

Obviously sobered by Jesus' words, the disciples later ask, *Tell us, when will these things be? And what will be the sign of Your coming, and of the end of the age?* It was in response to this specific question concerning the sign of His coming and the end of the age that He warned, *Take heed that no one deceives you.*

That this would be His immediate response to their question underlines the fact that spiritual deception will be rampant at the time of the end. His answer expresses the need for vigilance on the part of His followers, so as not be taken in by the false spirituality that will characterize those times.

Jesus then proceeded to warn, *For many will come in my name, saying, "I am the Christ" and will deceive many*. The word "Christ" is from the Greek word *christos* and literally means "anointed one" and refers to someone with a special, divine call or assignment from God. It is the Greek word that is used for the Hebrew "Messiah," which is why it is associated with Jesus.

This warning by Jesus indicates that the last days will be characterized by people falsely claiming to have a special, divine assignment or "anointing" from God to do what they are doing. In other words, those with a messianic complex will be numerous at the time of the end.

In Matthew 24:11 Jesus again warns of false prophets at the time of the end, saying, *Then many false prophets will rise up and deceive many*. Many of these false prophets will be able to perform great signs and wonders, for in vs. 24 Jesus warns, *For false christs and false prophets will rise and show great signs and wonders to deceive, if possible, even the elect*.

John the Apostle Warns of Deception

John, who was there listening to Jesus that day, later wrote his own warnings about deception in the last days. In the Book of Revelation, John speaks of an individual at the end of the age whom he calls the "False Prophet" (Revelation 16:13; 19:20; 20:10). This "False Prophet" is a great religious leader who deludes the masses with miraculous signs and wonders.

Along with the Dragon (Satan) and the Beast (also known as "Antichrist"), they form a false, unholy trinity. As the role of the Holy Spirit is to draw people to Christ, the role of the "False Prophet" is to draw people to the Beast and cause the masses to worship the Beast and his image. He does this by performing great miraculous signs, even making fire come down from heaven on the earth. John says that it is by these miraculous signs that he *deceives those who dwell on the earth.*

This False Prophet is the summation and epitome of all the deception that has been ongoing since the serpent beguiled Eve in the Garden of Eden. The false spirit that drives him is the same spirit behind all the false religions that have arisen in the world and behind all the false prophets and sects that have arisen within Christendom.

This is borne out by John in his First Epistle where he refers to the partner of the False Prophet, who in Revelation he calls "the Beast," but in this Epistle, he calls "Antichrist." John writes,

> *You have heard that Antichrist is coming, even now many antichrists have come, by which we may know it is the last hour* (I John 2:18).

John is saying that although an individual "Antichrist" is yet to come, the antichrist spirit is already at work. As a result, John says, many antichrists have already come and are already at work in the world.

The same can be said of the False Prophet. Although there is an individual "False Prophet" predicted for the end of the age, the false spirituality he will embody is already at work in the world. John referred to this in I John 4:1 when he admonished his readers not to believe every spirit, but to test the spirits, *because many false prophets have gone out into the world.*

Paul Warns of Deceiving Spirits

Paul also taught that false signs and wonders will be part of the Antichrist system. In II Thessalonians 2:1-10 he refers to the Antichrist as the "man of sin" and the "lawless one." He then says that the coming of the "lawless one" will be, *According to the working of Satan, with all power, signs and lying wonders* (II Thessalonians 2:9).

Observing how many modern charismatics are so fascinated with miracles and so lacking in discernment, I have sometimes wondered if they would not be among the first to embrace the Antichrist when he comes on the scene with his signs and lying wonders.

In I Timothy 4:1 Paul indicates that this may be the case, for he speaks of the "latter times" being characterized by some departing from "the faith," having been led astray by "deceiving spirits." He writes,

> *Now the Spirit expressly says that in latter times some will depart from the faith giving heed to deceiving spirits and doctrines of demons.*

When Paul puts the definite article in front of "faith" so that it reads "the faith," he is speaking of the basic, essential truths necessary to make one a Christian. In this verse he warns that in the latter times some will depart from "the faith," *i.e.,* they will depart from the Gospel itself, having been led astray by deceiving spirits.

11

We Must be Prepared for These Days

Yes, it is an exciting time to be alive. God is at work throughout the earth. He is pouring out His Spirit on "all flesh." We must not, however, allow our excitement to become a giddiness wherein we lose sight of the seriousness of the moment. We must be alert as Peter warned in I Peter 5:8,

> *Be sober, be vigilant; because your adversary the devil walks about like a roaring lion seeking whom he may devour.*

We must remember that Satan does not come in a red suit, with horns and a pitchfork. He disguises himself and comes as an "angel of light." We must, therefore, be equipped to recognize him and his deceptive devices.

In the following pages we will learn many lessons from both Scripture and Christian history that will prepare us discern the true from the false and the fake from the real.

Chapter 2

Paul Confronts a False Prophetess in Philippi

"Some today would have told this young woman that her fortunetelling ability was a gift from God and that she merely needed to submit it to Him. That was not Paul's approach. He discerned that her gift was demonically inspired and he cast out the spirit that gave her that ability. When the demon went out, her fortunetelling powers were gone."

Eddie L. Hyatt

I had a strange encounter with a deceiving spirit while preaching my first "revival" meeting at the Assembly of God in Kiowa, Oklahoma in 1972. It happened one afternoon as two friends and I were going door to door, witnessing and inviting people to the meetings.

We knocked on a door and a strange but very "spiritual" little man invited us into his home. We immediately noticed that his walls were papered with pictures and letters from well-known preachers with whom he obviously corresponded and listened to on the radio.

Almost immediately he began telling us about his sensational, spiritual experiences. He had experienced, he said, visions and out-of-the-body experiences. He told us that he had been to both heaven and hell. He also said he saw Jesus in hell, whom he said was still there suffering for our sins.

At this point my friend, Ruel, interrupted and said, "Jesus is not in hell; He is in heaven." This individual angrily retorted, "Don't you call me a liar; I will kill you. I was there. I saw him."

From the beginning, our spirits did not witness with the spirit that was in this man. But what clinched it for us was when he said that he saw Jesus in hell suffering for our sins. This was so contradictory to what the New Testament says about Jesus ascending on high and sitting at the right hand of the Father that we immediately knew it was a lie and that he was possessed with a deceiving spirit.

We offered to pray for him and he accepted our offer. He was now seated in a chair and as we laid our hands on him he bowed his head and began jabbering in tongues. Suddenly, he lifted his head and began making strange motions with his hands toward us.

When my friend, Charles, asked what the hand gestures were all about, he replied, "When I put that on someone, they usually die within three days." We had no fear, but we departed realizing he did not really want deliverance and was taken captive by the deceiving spirit to which he had yielded himself.

The same deceiving spirit at work in that man was at work in Bible times. Paul encountered a similar spirit during his time of ministry in Philippi.

Paul Encounters a False, Deceptive Spirit

During their time of ministry in the city of Philippi of Macedonia, Paul and Silas encountered a young woman who prophesied through what Luke calls *a spirit of divination* (Acts 16:16). However, the Greek word from

14

which "divination" is translated is *python,* a word associated with prophecy amongst the ancient Greeks and Romans. Because it was so well known in the ancient Greco-Roman world, the original readers of Acts would have made an immediate association when they read the words "spirit of python."

Prophecy in the Ancient World

Prophecy was common among the ancient Greeks and Romans. In fact, the noted historian, F.C. Grant, has said that the consultation of prophetic oracles was probably the most universal cult practice in the Greco-Roman world.[2]

"Oracle" was a word used by the ancients for a message from the gods, *i.e.,* a prophecy. It was also used of the location where the oracles were given. Many regions had their own divinely inspired prophets or prophetesses who gave their oracles (prophecies) to a constant stream of seekers.

Prophecy was also common in the ancient pagan and mystery religions. This is borne out by the Roman historian, Livy (59 B.C. – A.D. 17), who describes followers of the pagan deity, Bacchus, who "as if insane, with fanatical tossings of their bodies, would utter prophecies." He also describes devotees of the goddess Cybele as "prophesying in their frenzied chants."[3]

---

[2] F. C. Grant, *Hellenistic Religions: The Age of Syncretism* (New York: Liberal Arts Press, n.d.), 33.

[3] Livy, *Annals,* vol. 11, trans. Evan T. Sage, *LCB,* ed. T.E. Page et. al. (Cambridge: Cambridge University, 1949), xxxix.12.12.

So pronounced was the public's fascination with the supernatural that Petronius, a first century Roman official and novelist, declared that, "It is easier to meet a god than a man."

That prophecy and the supernatural were so common in the ancient, pagan world is why there are so many admonitions in the New Testament to not be deceived; and is why Paul, every time he mentions prophecy, includes an admonition to judge, test and prove the genuineness of prophecy.

The Oracle at Delphi

The most famous ancient, pagan oracle (prophetic center) was at the city of Delphi in Greece and was known as the "Oracle at Delphi." According to legend, the Greek god, Apollo, had slain a large female serpent--a python--at that site and the spirit of the python had remained. According to the legend, it now possessed the prophets and prophetesses who functioned there, "taking possession of their organs of speech moving and compelling them to give prophetic utterances."[4]

This was commonly known as the "pythian spirit" or the "spirit of python." At the height of its popularity, the oracle at Delphi maintained three prophetesses who offered advice and counsel through the pythian spirit to a continual stream of visitors including generals and government officials. This is the association the first

---

[4] David Aune, *Prophecy in Early Christianity and the Ancient Mediterranean World* (Grand Rapids: Eerdmans, 1983), 33, 354.

readers of Acts would have made to Luke's mention of a "spirit of python."

One characteristic of the Oracle at Delphi—and all pagan prophecy—is that it was self-induced. Preceding their prophetic functions, the priestesses would go through ritual baths, sprinklings and animal sacrifices leading to a hyped and frenzied prophetic state.

One ancient drawing pictured the prophetess in a disheveled, frenzied state as she gave forth her oracle. Other pagan religions used music, dance, contortions and sex orgies to work themselves into a prophetic frenzy. (Do we charismatics have our own rituals by which we work ourselves into a "prophetic" state?)

How We Open Ourselves to a Spirit of Python

In contrast, New Testament prophecy is not self-induced, *i.e.*, it does not come forth at the initiative of the person prophesying. We do not work ourselves into a prophetic frenzy like the pagans. Paul is very clear in I Cor. 12:11 that the gifts of the Spirit, including prophecy, are given *as He [the Holy Spirit] wills*. Although we can learn about how prophecy and Spiritual gifts function, it is dangerous to think that we can learn "how to" prophesy of our own initiative.

This is, perhaps, why Paul allowed this situation with the young woman to go on for "many days" before dealing with it and casting out the spirit. He did not have a "how to" list for dealing with such situations but was dependent on the leading and guidance of the Holy Spirit.

I am convinced that when we begin to push ourselves into prophesying out of our own hearts, apart from the Holy Spirit, we open ourselves to false spirits such as the spirit of python that possessed this young woman in Philippi.

We Must Recognize the Counterfeit

Some today would have told this young woman that her fortunetelling ability was a gift from God and that she merely needed to submit it to Him. That was not Paul's approach. He discerned that her gift was demonically inspired and he cast out the spirit that gave her that ability. When the demon went out, her fortunetelling powers were gone.

David Brainerd (1718-1747) ministered to Native Americans with great success. He tells of a medicine man among the Delaware who was feared and held in high esteem by the people because of his psychic and miracle working abilities. Brainerd said that when he preached about the miracles of Jesus being evidence of His divinity, the people were not impressed and proceeded to tell him about this man and his supernatural powers.

The medicine man eventually came to hear Brainerd preach and was powerfully convicted by the Holy Spirit and eventually accepted Christ as His Lord and Savior. Like the young woman, when she was delivered of the python spirit, he immediately lost all his supernatural powers. His testimony was, "When the word of God came into my heart, the power I had known went out."

His conversion and testimony had a powerful impact on the Delaware and other tribes in the region.

A person born into a family that practices palm reading, tarot card readings, ouija boards and other occultic practices may develop natural or soulish psychic abilities. They may also pick up demons, or what the Old Testament calls "familiar spirits." It is a grave mistake to think that these are God-given gifts that will hopefully be submitted to God. They are demonic counterfeits of the true workings of the Holy Spirit and must be renounced and cast out.

Characteristics of a Spirit of Python

Luke uses "spirit of python" in regards to this slave girl probably because the spirit operating in her was like the one at Delphi. There is, of course, the possibility that she had actually been to Delphi and that is where she picked up this false spirit.

It is important to note that what she said was true. Satan and demons have some knowledge and will reveal their "secrets" in order to impress and draw people into their destructive web. Only our God, however, is omniscient, *i.e.*, all knowing.

Here are some of the traits of a spirit of python that are obvious in this narrative.

- **It loves to flatter.** The prophecy of this young woman was not given to encourage or affirm, but to flatter. We all need to give and receive affirmation and encouragement, but flattery is insincere and self-serving. So many today, including leaders, are so starved for affirmation and approval that they are vulnerable to the flatteries of a deceiving, python spirit. We must be so settled in God's acceptance and approval that we are no longer susceptible to the flatteries of a false prophetic spirit. Beware of those who use prophecy to flatter and, thereby, gain advantage.

- **It demands attention.** This is indicated by the fact that she followed Paul and the others for "many days" continually giving forth her prophecy. Beware of those who use prophecy to thrust themselves into the limelight.

- **It loves to be seen and heard.** This is indicated by the fact that she kept putting herself at the center of attention. Note those who use prophecy to make themselves the center of attention.

- **It wants to be important.** This is indicated by the fact that she directed her prophesying to the leaders of this new movement. Beware of those who use prophecy to gain status with pastors and leaders.

- **There is a monetary motive.** This young slave girl was raking in a lot of money for her masters. I am afraid this same motive is at work in the charismatic/prophetic movement today. Some brashly offer a personal prophecy in return for a financial gift. Others are more subtle. I once saw a man, who probably was used in a genuine gift of prophecy, express his desire to pray for everyone who would bring a certain offering for his ministry to the front. As he prayed and then prophesied over each one, I saw women looking in their purses for money so they could go forward and "get a word." I believe this man was opening himself to a false spirit—a spirit of python—by his devious actions.

Taking A Stand for Truth

There is so little discernment today that many churches in the modern charismatic/prophetic movement would probably have put this young woman on their prophetic team, for what she prophesied was accurate and positive.

Discernment is lacking because, in this post-modern world, the lines between true and false are being blurred and even erased. Reason and common sense are being replaced by a me-centered philosophy that creates its own reality.

Some in the charismatic movement are tapping into New Age writings with the excuse that "all truth is God's truth." If this had been Paul's approach he would never have confronted the python spirit and cast it out, for what was being said was true.

Taking a stand for truth is not always the most popular thing to do. Paul and Silas were arrested, beaten and thrown in jail because they distinguished between the true and the false and cast out the python spirit. Nonetheless, they refused to compromise truth and God sent an earthquake, physically and spiritually, and turned the situation completely around.

God is looking for people who will stand for truth in this hour. Truth is vital for it is our ultimate weapon against the "father of lies." This is why Jesus said,

> *If you abide in My word, you are My disciples indeed. And you shall know the truth, and the truth shall make you free* (John 8:31-32).

Chapter 3

5 Warning Signs That a Prophetic Movement Has Gone Awry

"Everything that he so boldly professed from the prophets and prophetesses, he, in the end, found it all falsehood and deception."

Obe Philips (1500-1568)

Winston Churchill once said, "Those who do not learn from history are doomed to repeat it." This is especially true of the church where the same mistakes have been made generation after generation concerning revival and the prophetic.

The following information is drawn from a document written around 1560 by Obe Philips, a leader in the sixteenth century Anabaptist movement that sought the restoration of New Testament Christianity. Philips was commissioned as an "apostle" in this movement and he commissioned others to this "office."

The document, entitled "Confessions," describes events in Europe in the 1530s. From this document I have delineated 5 warning signs from their experience that can help us avoid the tragic mistakes that produced such great suffering and distress for them.

Warning Sign #1
When Prophecy is Used to Enhance the Status of a Movement or an Individual

1517-1537 was a very exciting time for many Christians in Europe. A great spiritual reformation was under way and many believed that God was restoring the church to its original purity and power. Many believed that out of this restoration would come a great revival and harvest that would usher in the coming of the Lord and the end of the age.

In the midst of this end-time, revival atmosphere, individuals began to arise proclaiming themselves to be special end-time apostles and prophets, endowed by God with miraculous power to usher in His kingdom upon the earth.

One of the most prominent of these "apostles" was Melchoir Hoffman, a powerful preacher and teacher who gained a large following. His status was further enhanced when a prophetess saw in a vision a large white swan, larger and more beautiful than all the others, swimming in a beautiful river. She claimed it was revealed to her that the swan was Hoffman and that he represented the fulfillment of God's promise in Malachi 4:5 to send Elijah before the coming of the great and dreadful day of the Lord.

Biblical Insight: Satan plays on human ego and pride. God calls us to humble ourselves before Him and promises that He will then raise us up. Demons, on the other hand, tell us how great, wonderful, and significant we are in ourselves. The "Elijah" prophecy given to

Hoffman is one that Satan has used again and again to bring good men down because of pride.

The ultimate goal of prophecy is to point people to Jesus. This was confirmed by the heavenly being who was at John's side as they observed the vast heavenly host worshipping and praising God. Overwhelmed at the sight, John fell at the feet of his heavenly escort to worship him, who stopped him and said,

> See that you do not do that! I am your fellow servant, and of your brethren who have the testimony of Jesus. Worship God! **For the testimony of Jesus is the spirit of prophecy** (Revelation 19:10).

In John 16:13 Jesus said that when the Holy Spirit would come, *He will glorify Me, for He will take of what is mine and declare it to you.* The Holy Spirit is here to point people to Jesus. When people use prophecy to put themselves and their own movement on a pedestal, it is time to beware.

Warning Sign #2
When Prophecy Becomes the Primary Means for Determining the Will of God

Another individual prophesied that Hoffman would be imprisoned for six months in the city of Strasbourg, and after that, his ministry would spread over the whole world. Based on the prophecy, Hoffman moved to Strasbourg where he began to preach and teach throughout that city.

The first part of the prophecy was fulfilled when the Strasbourg authorities arrested Hoffman and had him imprisoned. Philips says that he entered the prison "willingly, cheerfully, and well comforted," convinced that the latter part of the prophecy would now soon come to pass.

While in prison, Hoffman wrote many letters which Philips says came every day describing "how his actions, his visions and revelations affected him." One individual prophesied that at the end of his six-month imprisonment, Hoffman would depart Strasbourg with 144,000 true apostles endowed with such miraculous power that no one would be able to resist them. Elated with such prophetic predictions, Hoffman vowed that he would take no food other than bread and water until the time of his deliverance.

Six months passed, however, and he was not released. More time elapsed and he found it necessary to break his fast. Hoffman eventually died in prison, a very disillusioned man. Philips says;

> Everything that he so boldly professed from the prophets and prophetesses, he, in the end, found it all falsehood and deception, in fact and in truth; and he was so deceived with all their visions, prophecies, commission, dreams, and Elijah role that my heart today feels pity for him on account of this distress of his soul.

Biblical Insight: It is clear from Scripture that personal prophecy is not for giving direction in life. There is not a single positive example of such in the New Testament. The only example of a personal prophecy giving direction is in Acts 21:4 where certain disciples, *by the*

Spirit, told Paul, who was on his way to Jerusalem, *not to go up to Jerusalem*. What did Paul do? He ignored what they said and continued on to Jerusalem. Prophecy must confirm what we already know in our heart and Paul had already *purposed in the Spirit* to go to Jerusalem (Acts 19:21).

Warning Sign #3
When Prophecy is Preoccupied
With Images, Numbers, and Symbols

Prophetic dreams and visions flourished in this movement. These dreams and visions predicted many remarkable things related to the establishing of God's kingdom and the destruction of the wicked. Much of this information was given in symbolic form which had to be interpreted by those who were "spiritual." Philips says,

> One came dragging a wagon without wheels, another wagon had three wheels, one wagon had no shaft, some no horses, some no recognizable driver, some had but one leg, some were lepers and beggars, some wore a tunic or a cloak with a lappet of fur. All this they could interpret for the brethren in a spiritual sense.

These prophecies, dreams and visions predicted remarkable successes for the people of God, including a super-empowerment of the Spirit by which they would be enabled to overcome the wicked and establish the kingdom of God in the earth. In his very moving account of these matters, Philips says,

Now when these teachings and consolation with all the fantasies, dreams, revelations and visions daily occurred among the brethren, there was no little joy and expectation among us, hoping all would be true and fulfilled, for we were all unsuspecting, innocent, simple, without guile or cunning, and were not aware of any false visions, prophets, and revelations.

Biblical Insight: In the New Testament God communicates very clearly and precisely to His people. When He spoke to Ananias in a vision about going and praying for Paul, God gave precise instructions (Acts 9:10-12). He told Ananias the name of the man he was to pray for, the name of the man in whose house Paul was staying and the precise street address. When God does speak in a symbol or image, it is for the purpose of communicating a more clear and vivid message. It is never done as a riddle that must be searched out and solved. God wants to communicate clearly with His children.

Warning Sign #4
When Those Prophesying are not Open to Testing and/or Correction

During this time, two new apostles arrived in Philips' home town of Leeuwarden. They declared that they had been commissioned to the apostolic office with such signs, miracles and workings of the Spirit that words failed them to describe it. They also declared that, "In a short time God would rid the earth of all shedders of blood and all tyrants and the godless."

Philips says that they frightened the people so that no one dared speak against them for fear they would be speaking against the commission and ordination of God. He says, "For we were all guileless children and had no idea that our own brethren would betray us."

Biblical Insight: False prophets are unteachable and unwilling for their prophecies to be evaluated and tested, as Scripture commands. Virtually every time New Testament Scriptures speak of prophecy, they also speak of evaluating and testing the prophecy, which is the responsibility of every believer. I Thessalonians 5:19-21, for example, says, *Do not quench the Spirit. Do not despise prophecies. Test all things; hold fast what is God.* I Corinthians 14:29 says, *Let two or three prophets speak and let the others judge.* And in this same vein of thought, I John 4:1 says, *Beloved, do not believe every spirit, but test the spirits, whether they are of God; because many false prophets have gone out into the world.*

Sign #5
When Prophecy Becomes a Replacement for the Scriptures and Common Sense

The tragic end of this prophetic movement came, when based on dreams, visions, prophecies, and supposed angelic visitations, a number of these visionaries claimed that God had designated the city of Munster as the *New Jerusalem* and from there the kingdom of God would spread through all the earth. Philips says, "Some had spoken with God, others with angels—until they got a new trek under way to Munster." Based on the prophecies and supposed visions, they went to Munster and took the city by force from the Catholics who controlled it and renamed it *New Jerusalem*.

The Catholics, however, quickly regrouped and regained control of the city. They wasted no time in inflicting a terrible slaughter on those apostles, prophets and their followers who believed they were setting up the kingdom of God on the earth.

Philips tells about going to Munster and walking among the bodies, many of them beheaded, of these individuals who had been his friends and acquaintances. It was a very somber time and a wake-up call for him as he observed the sad end of these apostles and prophets who had relied without question on their dreams, visions and prophecies.

This whole fiasco resulted in widespread persecution of all Anabaptists who were hunted down, imprisoned, hanged, burned, and drowned. Philips later lamented his role in the extremes of this movement. He wrote,

> It is this which is utter grief to my heart and which I will lament before my God as long as I live, before all my companions, as often as I think of them. At the time that I took leave of those brethren, I had warned Menno and Dietrich and declared my [apostolic] commission unlawful and that I was therein deceived. I thank the gracious and merciful God who opened my eyes, humbled my soul, transformed my heart, captured my spirit, and who gave me to know my sins. And when I still think of the resigned suffering which occurred among the brethren, my soul is troubled and terrified before it.

Biblical Insight: In Psalm 119:105 David said, *Your word is a lamp to my feet and a light to my path.* When Jesus was tempted by Satan in the wilderness to doubt His identity, He responded to each temptation with, *It is written,* and then quoted the appropriate passage of Scripture. John Wesley, who saw many unusual spiritual manifestations as the leader of the eighteenth-century Methodist revival, said, "Try all things by the written word, and let all bow down before it."

Conclusion

This sixteenth century prophetic movement highlights the need to "test the spirits" and to "judge" prophetic utterances according to the Scriptures. For the most part, these were sincere, seeking people who suffered much pain, grief and even death because they neglected this Biblical admonition. May we learn from their example and not repeat their mistakes.

Chapter 4

When Satan Comes As an Angel of Light

*For such are false apostles, deceitful workers, transforming themselves
into apostles of Christ. And no wonder! For Satan himself transforms
himself into an angel of light.*

II Corinthians 11:13-14

Did you know that the early Mormons experienced speaking in tongues, prophecy, falling under the power, visions, and angelic visitations? Did you know that this movement, that denies the virgin birth of Jesus and believes there are many gods ruling different plants, emerged out of one of the most powerful revivals in Christian history, the Second Great Awakening? In fact, an examination of their beginnings reveals many similarities with the modern charismatic-prophetic movement.

Their example is a wake-up call for all who embrace the supernatural ministry of the Holy Spirit to be diligent in carrying out the Biblical commands to test the spirits and to judge prophetic utterances and supernatural manifestations. After all, Satan does not come in a red suit with horns and a pitchfork; he comes as an angel of light (II Corinthians 11:14).

Peter Cartwright's Autobiography

Peter Cartwright (1786was a circuit-riding Methodist preacher and one of the most remarkable revivalists of the Second Great Awakening. His autobiography offers intriguing reading and provides valuable information concerning the religious landscape in early and mid-nineteenth century America.

His autobiography also offers a personal glimpse into the origins of Mormonism and how it began in the milieu of religious revivalism. His account, which includes interactions with Joseph Smith, provides an historical example of the dangers of naively embracing everything sensational and the importance of obeying the Biblical injunction to test the spirits and to judge prophetic utterances and spiritual manifestations.

The Mormons Speak in Tongues

Cartwright tells about a large campmeeting he was conducting with thousands in attendance, including Methodists, Baptists, Presbyterians, Quakers and others. On Saturday morning, he said, "There came some twenty or thirty Mormons to the meeting. "

He tells how at the end of the service, the Mormons remained behind, singing and praising God. They were excellent singers and many began coming back under the tabernacle to hear them. They continued singing and as people finished their noon meal they came back to the tabernacle until there was a large crowd gathered around them.

Eventually one of the Mormon women in this group began to shout and then swooned away and fell into the arms of her husband. Her husband then announced that she was in a trance and that when she came out of it she would speak in an unknown tongue and he would interpret. This was obviously not something new for them.

Cartwright, by this time, decided to break up their meeting, as he believed they were purposely seeking to draw attention to themselves. As he walked into the midst of the group the woman in the trance began speaking in tongues. When Cartwright told her to "hush," she opened her eyes, laid her hand on his arm, and said, "Dear friend, I have a message directly from God to you."

Cartwright, who was a gruff sort of personality, said, "I stopped her short and said, 'I will have none of your message.'" The woman's husband, who was to interpret the message in tongues, angrily replied, "Sir this is my wife, and I will defend her at the risk of my life." Cartwright retorted, "Sir, this is my campmeeting and I will maintain the good order of it at the risk of my life ."[5]

After an exchange of emotionally charged words, the group finally left. Cartwright identified them as Mormons, followers of a "Joe Smith" with whom he had had several conversations.

Cartwright Meets "Joe" Smith

Cartwright had several meetings with the founder of Mormonism, Joseph Smith, whom he called "Joe Smith." Smith shared with him his vision for the restoration of the church of the New Testament. According to Smith, during a time of revival in upper state New York he had prayed about which church was the right one. Smith said that during this time of prayer, I saw a pillar of light

---

[5] W.P. Strickland, ed., *Autobiography of Peter Cartwright, The Backwoods Preacher,* 344.

exactly over my head, above the brightness of the sun, which descended gradually until it fell upon me. When the light rested upon me I saw two Personages, whose brightness and glory defy all description, standing above me in the air.[6]

According to Smith, the Father, Son and Holy Spirit appeared in this vision and told him not to join any of the churches, for none was the true church.

Cartwright says that Smith, at first, sought to flatter him telling him how privileged he was to meet him and saying that, of all the churches then in existence, the Methodist church was the closest to the church of the New Testament. According to Smith, however, the Methodists had stopped short by not claiming the gift of tongues, of prophecy, and of miracles. He went on to tell Cartwright,

> If you will go with me to Nauvoo (a Mormon community), I will show you many living witnesses that will testify that they were, by the saints, cured of blindness, lameness, deafness, dumbness, and all the diseases that human flesh is heir to. And I will show you that we have the gift of tongues, and can speak in unknown languages, and that the saints can drink any deadly poison and it will not hurt them.[7]

---

[6] Ruth Tucker, *Another Gospel* (Grand Rapids: Zondervan, 2004), 51.

[7] W.P. Strickland, ed., *Autobiography of Peter Cartwright, The Backwoods Preacher* (New York: Carlton & Porter, 1857), 343.

Cartwright said that when he did not respond to the flattery and began to question Smith about his doctrine, Smith changed his tactic. Smith then began to warn him not to resist a good work of God and to say how it was "an awful thing to fight against God."

Smith Proves to be Angry and Unteachable

As Cartwright continued to question Smith about his doctrine, it soon became obvious that Smith had left behind Biblical truth and was following sensational teachings based on prophecies, visions, and supposed angelic visitations.

As Cartwright continued pointing out his error, he said that Smith's wrath boiled over and "he cursed me in the name of his God." Smith angrily retorted,

> I will show you, sir, that I will raise up a government in these United States which will overturn the present government, and I will raise up a new religion that will overturn every other form of religion in this country.[8]

Visions & Angelic Visitations

Joseph Smith and his early followers not only claimed the miraculous gifts of the Spirit, they claimed to experience visions and angelic visitations on a regular basis. Those of the contemporary prophetic movement would have, if they had been there, designated Smith as a prophet or seer.

---

[8] W.P. Strickland, ed., *Autobiography of Peter Cartwright, The Backwoods Preacher*, 345.

On one occasion an angel that Smith called Moroni supposedly appeared to him and told him where to find the plates on which were inscribed the Book of Mormon, written in an ancient Egyptian text. Smith claimed that while he and an associate, Oliver Cowdery, were translating the book, John the Baptist as well as Peter, James, and John appeared to them and ordained them to the priesthood of Melchizedek.

How impressive! Demons will always play on human credulity and pride, telling them how important they will be if they accept this revelation.

The Dedication of the First Mormon Temple

In 1831, based on a supposed revelation from God, Smith and many of his followers migrated to Kirkland, Ohio. There they built, and in 1836, dedicated the first Mormon temple. According to one Mormon historian, there was a spiritual outpouring almost unmatched in ecclesiastical history. Smith himself wrote a detailed description.

> A noise was heard like the sound of a rushing mighty wind, which filled the Temple, and all the congregation simultaneously arose, being moved upon by an invisible power; many began to speak in tongues and prophesy; others saw glorious visions; and I beheld the Temple filled with angels, which fact I declared to the congregation. The people of the neighborhood came running (hearing an unusual sound within, and seeing a bright light like a pillar of fire resting on the Temple), and were astonished at what was taking

place. This continued until the meeting closed at eleven P.M.[9]

As can be clearly seen, Smith's description of this dedication could easily be the description of a modern charismatic/prophetic gathering. What we see here is probably a combination of exaggeration on the part of Smith, soulish hype in the dedication of the temple and angels of light mimicking the true demonstrations of the Holy Spirit.

What We Can Learn from Mormonism

Out of this group that based its beliefs on prophecies, visions, and angelic visitations, has grown a movement that today numbers millions of followers around the world. While many of their beliefs are obviously Christian in origin, they also hold to many beliefs that have no basis in Scripture and are at odds with Biblical Christianity.

For example, Mormons teach a form of polytheism, claiming that the planets of the universe are ruled by different gods and that Elohim—the God of the Old Testament—is the god of this planet. They also teach that Elohim had a wife who bore his offspring as the Eternal Mother. According to Mormon doctrine, Jesus is merely the oldest of the offspring produced by the Heavenly Father and Heavenly Mother, and we are all his spirit brothers and sisters.[10]

---

[9] Ruth Tucker, *Another Gospel*, 61

[10] Tucker, *Another Gospel*, 82.

Their strange doctrines, and practices such as baptizing for the dead and polygamous marriage, came forth because they exalted their spiritual experiences and writings, such as the Book of Mormon, to equal status with, and even above, the Bible. This happened because they failed to "test the spirits" and judge the prophecies and visions in their midst as Scripture commands. Interestingly, Cartwright, regarded the Mormons as a living example of Satan's ability to transform himself into an "angel of light."

Here are some suggestions that can help us avoid repeating the same mistakes as this movement.

1) **Make the diligent study of God's word our number one priority.** Anything can be proved by proof-texting, *i.e.,* quoting verses of Scripture out of context. Let the Bereans of Acts 17:11 be our guide. They were commended because, instead of naively accepting what Paul and Silas preached, *they searched the Scriptures daily to find out whether those things were so.*

2) **Don't be afraid to "test the spirits."** We will not quench the Holy Spirit by doing what He has commanded us to do. We may quench spiritual pride and religious ambition, but not the Holy Spirit. Smith and the early Mormons did not test the spirits, nor did they judge their prophetic-supernatural experiences. Instead they twisted Scripture to make it fit their experience. Avoid this at all costs.

3) **Stop chasing the sensational.** Let the supernatural happen: Don't try to make it happen. The early Mormons were obviously enamored with the sensational—visions, angelic visitations, and so on. This led to their departure from Biblical truth. Along with teaching the miraculous dimension of our Christian faith, we must emphasize the practical Christian lifestyle of Scripture. This is clearly articulated in passages such as the Sermon on the Mount. Don't be afraid of using some sanctified common sense, which the Bible calls wisdom.

4) **Avoid spiritual pride.** Stop trying to be important and simply be obedient to the Lord. Peter Cartwright says that Smith told him that if he [Cartwright] would join him [Smith], "We could sweep, not only the Methodist church, but all the churches, and you would be looked up to as one of the Lord's greatest prophets." Do you see and hear the pride in that statement? Remember that, "the stronghold of deception is pride."

5) **Avoid an elitist mindset.** Smith claimed that he and his followers were the true restored church of the New Testament and that all other churches were false churches (the Mormons still believe this). This too was based on pride and an unhealthy lust for importance and power.

My Prayer

My prayer is that God will have mercy on us, and bless us, and cause His face to shine upon us, that His ways may be known upon earth and His salvation among all nations (Psalm 67). May God give us a love and hunger for His word, a sharpened sense of discernment, and the courage to speak and walk in His truth. Amen!

Chapter 5

The Stronghold of Deception

"As one rises higher and higher in spiritual power and blessing, he must ever seek to become lower and lower and lower and lower."

Gordon Lindsay

It was during the praise and worship service just before I was to preach in a very lively "revival" church. It was a very festive atmosphere with people shouting, waving banners and running the aisles. As I quietly worshipped, I heard the Holy Spirit say, "The stronghold of deception is pride."

I immediately knew that I was to address the fact, that during times of revival, pride often creeps in because of the power and blessing of God. Individuals and churches get an inflated sense of their own importance because of God's blessing on their lives. This pride then becomes an opening and a stronghold for demonic deception.

By the time I finished my message that morning, a solemn quietness had settled over the congregation. After the benediction, everyone seemed almost afraid to talk and spoke quietly and in whispers as they departed. It was such a contrast to the earlier festive atmosphere that I was somewhat concerned.

After the service, I shared with the pastor that I hoped I had not squelched the enthusiasm of his congregation. He replied, "Oh no, you were right on target." "In fact," he said, "I may be accused of bringing you in as a hired gun today."

He then shared how that the very thing I addressed that morning had been happening within his congregation. He told how individuals who had been saved less than a year in the revival had challenged his leadership. Because they were experiencing God, they had gotten an inflated sense of their own importance, not realizing that what they had experienced was out of God's goodness and grace.

God Resists the Proud

Gordon Lindsay, one of the most prominent leaders of the divine healing revivals of the 1940s-50s, declared, "As one rises higher and higher in spiritual power and blessing, he must ever seek to become lower and lower and lower and lower."

This statement was born out of his observation of the tragic collapse of the lives and ministries of several men who had been powerfully used of God in ministries of healing and deliverance. In each case, Satan's door of entry into the person's life seems to have been an inflated idea of his own importance.

Instead of humbling themselves before God, they became enamored with their own success. And instead of moving on to greater displays of God's glory and power, they were brought down because of their pride and arrogance. 1 Peter 5:5 says that God *resists the proud but gives grace to the humble.*

William Branham

For several years, beginning in 1947, Lindsay managed the ministry of William Branham, the most prominent healing evangelist of the 1940s-50s. Branham was launched into an amazing ministry of signs and wonders after an angel appeared to him during a time of prayer and instructed him to take a gift of healing to the people of the world.

Thousands attended his crusades because of the prominence of healings and miracles. These giant crusades were organized by Lindsay who also emceed the meetings and taught in the morning sessions.

When the time came for Branham to preach in the evening services, Lindsay would introduce him in a low-key manner while at the same time acknowledging that God was using him in a remarkable way.

How Branham Was Deceived

Once, when Lindsay was away, a "Brother Baxter" emceed the meetings and introduced Branham. His flowery introduction was filled with glowing accolades and he referred to Branham as a special "end-time prophet of God." When Lindsay returned, Branham said, "Brother Lindsay, I think I would like for Brother Baxter to introduce me from now on."[11]

---

[11] These facts were relayed to the author by the late Freda Lindsay, wife of Gordon Lindsay, who was privy to all the details described.

Branham then began to surround himself with individuals who fed his ego with ideas about being a special end-time prophet of God. Lindsay sought to warn him, but his advice was not heeded. When he saw that Branham had embraced serious error, he withdrew from Branham's ministry and developed the Voice of Healing, known today as Christ for the Nations.

Branham eventually began to believe that he was the fulfillment of God's promise in Malachi 4:5 which says, *I will send you Elijah the prophet before the coming of the great and dreadful day of the Lord*. He also identified himself with the angel of the seventh church in Revelation 3:14.

Branham went on to embrace and teach other bizarre doctrines. His "serpent seed" doctrine said that Eve's sin involved sexual relations with the serpent with people descended from this event and, therefore, destined for hell. Those who would receive his teachings were the seed of God and destined to become the bride of Christ.

In spite of his bizarre self-concept and erroneous teachings, miracles continued to occur in his meetings. God is merciful!

Kenneth Hagin's Prophecy

In 1963, Kenneth Hagin walked into Lindsay's office and handed him a prophecy which he had written out. The prophecy stated that the leader of the deliverance revival had gotten off track and would shortly be removed from the scene.

Lindsay read the prophecy aloud in the presence of his wife, Freda, and then locked it in his desk. Freda asked,

"Who is he talking about?" With great somberness he replied, "He is talking about Branham. He has gotten off track and thinks that he is Elijah."

Two years later, Lindsay received a call from out-of-state asking him to come and pray for Branham who had been in a car accident and was in serious condition. Because of his previous experiences, Lindsay felt that he was to leave the situation completely in the hands of God and he did not go. A few days later he received word that Branham had died.

Though sad and tragic, Branham's experience is not unique in the annals of Church history. Again and again, as God has visited His people in answer to their prayers, pride has crept in and the revival has been squelched, and it is still happening today.

Pride in the Pentecostal/Charismatic Camp

While ministering in a large urban area on the east coast, I picked up and scanned a tabloid that appeals primarily to Pentecostals and Charismatics. I was stunned by the arrogance and pride in the advertising that had been placed by churches and ministries.

There were not only charismatic prophets, apostles and bishops, there were also "covering apostles," "presiding apostles," "jurisdictional apostles," "archbishops," "prelates" (religious rulers) and even one individual who had designated herself as "her super eminence Apostle so and so."

I thought, "Can these individuals be followers of the One who made Himself of no reputation and washed the feet of His own disciples, a task performed in that culture only by household servants and slaves?" Can they be followers of the One who, in Matt. 23:6-12, warned His disciples about adopting honorific titles that would set themselves apart from other believers.

> But you, do not be called "Rabbi"; for One is your Teacher, the Christ, and you are all brethren. Do not call anyone on earth your father; for One is your Father, He who is in heaven. And do not be called teachers; for One is your Teacher, the Christ. But he who is greatest among you shall be your servant.

No wonder the world does not see Jesus. They cannot see Jesus for us. No wonder we are not seeing a national spiritual awakening! The first condition for such an awakening, according to II Chronicles 7:14, is for the people of God to "humble themselves."

God Is Calling Us
to a Different Posture

Several years ago, I sat in a "Revival Now" conference and experienced an overwhelming urge to bow down before the Lord. I sat and contemplated what I should do for no one else was bowing down. In fact, people were going forward and standing as they waited to receive prayer for a fresh touch of the Holy Spirit.

However, as this urge to bow myself before the Lord continued, I finally turned and knelt at my seat. As soon as my knees touched the floor, I heard the Holy Spirit speaking in my heart in a clear and vivid manner. He said,

> I am going to be doing some incredible things in the days ahead: And when you see My power and My glory, this is to always be your posture. You are to bow down and acknowledge that I Am the sovereign Lord of this universe.

Yes, pride is the stronghold of deception. That is why we must continually acknowledge that it is not about us, but about Him. And remember the exhortation of Peter in I Peter 5:5b-6 where he said,

> *And be clothed with humility, for God resists the proud but gives grace to humble. Therefore, humble your selves under the mighty hand of God that He may exalt you in due time.*

Chapter 6

Learning to Distinguish Between Soul and Spirit

"I dislike something that has the appearance of enthusiasm, overvaluing feelings and inward impressions; mistaking the mere work of imagination for the voice of the Spirit."

John Wesley

A would-be "prophet" gave me a prophetic word concerning my "little brother" about whom, he said, I had been very concerned. He assured me there was no need for my concern. God, he said, had revealed to him that my little brother would be saved.

Now, there was only one problem with this prophecy: I do not have a little brother! When I shared this fact with this individual he seemed to be embarrassed and replied, "I will have to be more careful."

The sad thing was that the very next day I heard him giving detailed personal prophecies to people, even about God sending them to specific nations. I shook my head in disbelief, and for the sake of the people, thought to myself, "I hope you test what you are hearing."

He was not a false prophet, but simply a zealous individual who had never learned to distinguish between his soul and spirit. The prophecy was neither from God nor the devil, but had been formulated in his own soul, *i.e.*, his mind and emotions. It was the product of an overactive imagination, perhaps motivated by a desire for importance. This is why we must learn to distinguish between soul and spirit.

Discerning Between Soul & Spirit

There are three possible sources for a prophecy or spiritual manifestation: (1) From the Holy Spirit who dwells in the reborn spirit of the believer; (2) from a demonic spirit; (3) from the human soul, *i.e.*, the mind, will and emotions. I am convinced that many, if not most, of the prophecies we are hearing from Christians today are from neither God or the devil but are from the human soul.

It is, therefore, of utmost importance that we learn to distinguish between soul and spirit. The New Testament teaches that there is a difference between the human soul and the human spirit.

The spirit is the innermost part of our being and is that part that is regenerated when we are born again. It is through our human spirit that we have an awareness of God and the spirit realm. In born-again believers, the spirit is the place where the Holy Spirit dwells and, therefore, the place from which gifts of the Holy Spirit originate and flow.

The soul, on the other hand, consists of our mind, will, and emotions. It is the seat of the personality—the ego— and is that part of our being that gives us self-awareness. The soul, *i.e.*, mind, will, and emotions, can be moved by a variety of outward stimuli.

Good music, for example, has the power to stir positive emotions of love, nostalgia, and compassion apart from the Holy Spirit. Likewise, a gifted orator can stir emotions and move people to behave in ways they otherwise would not.

These, however, are mere feelings of the soul and have nothing to do with the Holy Spirit. By way of example, I can recall sitting in a restaurant and hearing an old secular song that brought back nostalgic memories of my childhood and family who are gone. It stirred my emotions even to the point of tears. This had nothing to do with the Spirit of God, but was occurring in my soul, *i.e.*, my mind and emotions.

Although some think of the soul and spirit as being the same, the New Testament makes a clear distinction between the two. In I Thessalonians 5:23, for example, Paul says, *May your whole spirit, soul, and body be preserved blameless at the coming of* our *Lord Jesus Christ*. Hebrews 14:12 clearly says that the soul and spirit are two distinct entities and that only the Word of God can divide the two. Making a distinction between soul and spirit can be very helpful in discerning the source of a manifestation.

Our spirit is sometimes referred to in Scripture as "the heart." For example, Jesus was speaking of the human spirit when He said, *He who believes on Me, as the Scripture has said, out of his heart will flow rivers of living water* (John 7:38). Jesus was speaking of the Holy Spirit who would dwell in those who believe in Him and from whom would flow gifts of the Holy Spirit.

Those who are zealous to be used of God and see His power, will often mistake the stirring of their emotions for the Holy Spirit. This is what John Wesley was referring to, when on October 29, 1762, he cautioned a colleague who was mistaking his own thoughts and imaginations for the Holy Spirit. Wesley said;

> I dislike something that has the appearance of enthusiasm, overvaluing feelings and inward impressions; mistaking the mere work of imagination for the voice of the Spirit, and undervaluing reason, knowledge, and wisdom in general.[12]

Many today mistake emotional highs for the presence of God. Many "revival" services are nothing more than skilled musicians and a savvy preacher stirring people's emotions. R. A. Torrey (1856-1928) was referring to such "soulish" revivals when he wrote,

> The most fundamental trouble with most of our present-day, so called revivals is, that they are man-made and not God sent. They are worked up (I almost said faked up) by man's cunningly devised machinery—not prayed down.[13]

Soulish Prophecies

A roommate in Bible school shared with me about a puzzling and discouraging experience he had with prophecy. He had gone with a small group to pray for a woman who was in the last stages of terminal cancer. As they stood around the bed and prayed, he sensed what he believed was God's presence and he prophesied to the sick woman that God had heard her prayer and was healing her.

---

[12] Wesley, vol. 3 of *The Works of John Wesley*, 98.
[13] Torrey, *The Power of Prayer and the Prayer of Power*, 62.

He really felt the prophecy was from God, but just a few days later she died. He was embarrassed and confused. How could this happen? How could he have been so wrong?

I could share numerous stories like this where well-meaning people have given what they sincerely believed was a word from God, but that word turned out to be false. These are usually well-meaning people who desire to be used of God but have never learned to distinguish between their soul and their spirit.

The young man, Emile, whom I mentioned above, did not distinguish between soul and spirit in the prophecy he gave. No doubt, his natural feelings and emotions were moved by seeing the woman lying in bed and dying of cancer. He believed in Divine healing and desired so much to see a miracle of healing.

These, however, were natural feelings of the soul and not from the Spirit of God. He was moved out of his own natural feelings to give the prophecy. He gave what I call a "soulish" prophecy—a prophecy borne out of one's own feelings and emotions. He was not a false prophet, just a mistaken one.

Prophecy Must Be Initiated by the Spirit

Contrary to the biblical model, some teach that believers can prophesy at their own volition or will. I heard one well-known "prophet" insist that, just as it took Pentecostals several decades to discover that they could speak or pray in tongues at will, many in the body of Christ are now discovering that they can prophesy at will.

Proponents of this teaching point to the fact, that in 1 Corinthians 14:15, Paul says, "I will pray with the spirit," an obvious reference to praying in tongues. They give emphasis to the "I will" in this passage and reason that if one can will to pray or speak in tongues, then one can also will to prophesy.

This is poor hermeneutics and ignores the context of Paul's discussion. When Paul says, "I will pray with the spirit," he is referring to the private, devotional tongues in which he wills, or chooses, to pray. He distinguishes between private, devotional tongues in which he prays at will and the public manifestation of tongues that requires interpretation and comes forth as the Spirit wills, a very important distinction.

The idea that one can prophesy at will has resulted in many "prophets" operating out of their soul realm (mind, will and emotions) rather than from the Spirit. I have observed individuals who had become very adept at "reading" people and then giving a word that the recipient could easily apply to his or her own situation.

When this approach is coupled with immaturity or an unsavoury character, it becomes extremely dangerous with the prophet often prophesying to impress and manipulate others and to enhance his own standing. At this point, the one prophesying has crossed the dividing line from Christian prophecy, with its source in the Holy Spirit, to fortune-telling and psychic phenomena, with their sources in the human psyche and possibly the demonic.

Soulish Dreams & Visions

Shortly after Sue and I married and moved to Canada, I awakened in the night having had a very frightening dream that my father back in Texas had died. As I lay in the darkness thinking on the dream, I noted a clear and distinct sense down in my spirit that the dream was a lie, and I turned over and went back to sleep. And, sure enough, it was a lie for my father had many good years after that.

That dream, as are most dreams, occurred in the realm of the soul. It was the result of thoughts, feelings and anxiety in my psyche that were expressed during sleep in the form of a dream. It also could have been a thought or image put there by Satan for Scripture is clear that the mind and emotions are major battlefields with the enemy of our souls.

Whatever its source, it was not from God and when I awakened I had such a clear sense of distinction between my soul and my spirit, and an acute awareness that the dream occurred in the realm of the soul and was not from God.

God can and does speak through dreams, but that is not His normal way of speaking and guiding. The current faddish preoccupation with dreams and dream interpretation is not based in Scripture.

The idea that every dream is a message from God that must be interpreted is not from Jesus and the New Testament but is drawn from pagan New Age teachings and from occultic psychologists like Carl Jung. The only people in Scripture who needed their dream interpreted were pagan rulers in the Old Testament.

Most dreams are soulish, *i.e.*, the natural workings of our mind and emotions sorting out concerns, desires, fears, hopes and anxieties while we sleep. If you have a dream that is from God, you will know it in your spirit and most likely will immediately know its meaning.

Soulish Revival

In 1974 my two young friends and I attended a revival meeting in which one of the well-known healing evangelists of the 1950s was speaking. We had read his book and had been greatly stirred by his stories of faith and miracles, which is why we were willing to drive over one hundred miles to be in his meeting in a church in Dallas, Texas. It turned out to be a disappointing time.

The church was pastored by another well-known evangelist from the 1950s. They met in a former movie theatre with theater style seating and long aisles between the seats.

This individual whom we had come to hear walked slowly down the aisles continuously talking and calling on people to stand in the aisle where he would then pray for them and prophesy to them. We noted that he was treating people quite roughly as he laid his hands on them and pushed them to the floor.

He eventually came our way and asked me to stand in the aisle. As I stood in front of him he said, "You are a preacher, aren't you?" I replied "yes." He then proceeded to give me a supposed prophetic word that was very generic, irrelative to my life and with no sense of life or power in it. He ended his prophecy and prayer by giving me a karate-like chop on both sides of my neck as he shouted "Hhhaaa!"

That was my cue to fall to the floor, but I didn't. I was knocked backwards, but not by the power of God! I put one foot back to keep from falling. The evangelist was obviously disgusted that I did not fall. He whirled around, and as he walked briskly up the aisle, said over the PA system, "Preachers are the hardest people in the world to pray for!"

There was no sense of God's peace or presence in any of this—just a preacher trying to impress people and make them think that God's power was working through him. Even as a young believer, I could see that many preachers, like this evangelist, who had once known the touch of God on their lives, were trying to continue in their soul realm what God had begun in them by His Spirit. I was getting an early lesson in the need to discern between the true and the false in revival and between the soul and the spirit.

The Necessity of Honesty & Integrity

In learning to distinguish between soul and spirit, honesty and integrity must be paramount even if we have to eat some humble pie along the way. We must not set ourselves up as some infallible voice of God and then try to justify ourselves when we miss it. If you are not totally convinced that a word you are sharing is from God, simply say, "I feel to share something with you" or "I sense God may be saying," etc.

Don't feel obligated to preface everything with "thus saith the Lord" or "the Lord would say unto thee," etc.

Too many Christian leaders make bold explicit prophecies and then try and save face by walking back what they said when the prophecy turns out to be false.

As we walk in honesty and integrity before God and people, our sense of discernment between soul and spirit will grow. Those individuals who operate out of the soul and are unwilling to admit it, end up with their ability to discern being blunted and dulled, or what Scripture calls a "seared conscience" (I Timothy 4:2).

The importance of walking in openness and truth was addressed by Paul in II Corinthians 4:2 when he wrote,

> We reject all shameful deeds and underhanded methods. We don't try to trick anyone or distort the word of God. We tell the truth before God, and all who are honest know this (NLT).

Chapter 7

How to Think Critically Without Quenching the Spirit

Do you not know that the saints shall judge the world? And if the world shall be judged by you, are you unworthy to judge the smallest matters? Do you not know that we shall judge angels? How much more things that pertain to this life?

I Corinthians 6:2-3

The pastor invited me to preach on a Sunday morning and then alerted me that gold dust had been miraculously appearing in their services. My response was open but cautious. I was open because I value manifestations of the Holy Spirit, but cautious because there is no example of such a manifestation in Scripture, and Scripture is our primary guide for testing the spirits and judging manifestations.

I preached that Sunday morning, and as I was finishing my message, I noted that the children began coming from children's church into the auditorium to be with their parents. Almost immediately there was a commotion toward the back of the auditorium. I paused and someone announced, "The gold dust has appeared."

I politely acknowledged their excitement and concluded my message. Later, I was standing by my book table in the foyer of the church when I noticed the children's pastor coming toward me covered in gold dust. I asked, "What is that all over you?" She replied, "O we were playing with the glittery stuff in children's church today."

59

I immediately recalled that it was when the children came into the auditorium that the excitement erupted about the miraculous appearance of gold dust. I smiled and thought to myself, "I have discovered the source of their gold dust."

What it Means to "Think Critically"

Now, that was a harmless situation. However, if we are careless about "thinking critically" in the small things of life we will be careless in the larger things that could cost us our life.

This is what happened in 1978 when over 900 people, many of whom who had been members of evangelical and charismatic churches, followed a charismatic preacher—Jim Jones—to South America and committed mass suicide with him. It was a tragic and traumatic experience with many people crying as Jones shouted his order over the loud speakers for everyone to drink the poisonous cool-aid.

There were parents there with small children whose souls were in turmoil as they gave the poison to their children and then drank it themselves. What a tragedy! And one that could have been avoided if they had only been willing "think critically."

There were warning signs from the very beginning, such as his control over the personal lives of his followers and his egoism that was on full display. These warning signs, however, were ignored by his followers and it cost them their lives.

"Thinking critically" can, therefore, be life-saving. It is not about being negative or judgmental. "Criticism," in the academic sense, is defined by the Merriam-Webster Dictionary as "exercising or involving careful judgment or judicious evaluation." Therefore, to "think critically" is to question, consider and evaluate a situation or manifestation.

To "think critically" is an exercise of the mind. We are not to set aside or turn off our minds when it comes to the things of the Spirit. In Matthew 22:37, Jesus told us to love God with all our minds; and in Romans 12:2 Paul tells us that we will be transformed by the renewing of our minds. It is not the mind *per se*, that is the problem, it is the carnal mind, *i.e.*, the mind that has not been renewed in God's word.

Being Open Without Being Naive

Let me be clear in saying that I value spiritual gifts. I was catapulted into ministry forty-five years ago when a woman minister gave a powerful prophecy to a shy young man who could not speak in public but was carrying an intense call of God in his heart. That prophecy confirmed all that was in my heart and gave me the confidence I needed to step out in obedience to God's call.

About one year after this experience of being "launched," I was preaching an extended revival meeting in a church in Oklahoma. One night, after the meeting was over, a visiting preacher called me aside and spoke a word of prophecy over me. Although I don't remember what he said, I do remember the conversation with the pastor and his mother after the service as I rode with them to their home where I was staying.

They asked about the prophecy and what I thought about it. They then expressed their firm belief that God does not speak through personal prophecy. As we talked, the pastor, Jess, who was single and in his 50s, shared about a devastating experience he had with personal prophecy as a young man in his 20s.

He told about having a close friendship with a young woman who attended the same church as he and his family. Although they were not formally engaged, he loved her and thought she was probably the one he would someday marry.

She went away to spend the summer with relatives in another state. Toward the end of summer, a person at church asked, "Did you hear about Lois?" Jess replied, "No, I haven't heard from her." The person replied, "She got married."

Jess was shocked and devastated. How could this be? He learned later that in the church she attended with her relatives, a person prophesied to her that God had brought her there to marry a certain young man in the congregation. Wanting to obey God and not having been taught to question spiritual things, she and the young man married.

The marriage was an abject failure. Jess said that several years later, they divorced, and she returned to Oklahoma with three small children, very disillusioned with life and questioning aspects of her faith in God. Jess never married and passed away in his 70s.

Things could have been very different if they had understood the need to "think critically." Instead, Lois acted naively and accepted the prophecy without questioning it. Jess then reacted in the opposite direction and rejected all prophecy as a viable means of God speaking.

The Biblical Admonition to "Think Critically"

Yes, in these days, when spirituality and the supernatural are being emphasized, it is crucial that we also emphasize the importance of learning to "think critically." If we are to be protected from false, deceiving spirits, we must learn to "think critically."

This is not the same as the gift of discerning of spirits listed in I Corinthians 12:10. The gift of discerning of Spirits is a supernatural manifestation of the Holy Spirit whereby one is given the ability to clearly see the spirit at work in a person or a manifestation. It is not a permanent gift but is given at the discretion of the Holy Spirit for a particular time and situation.

To "think critically," on the other hand, is a human initiated exercise of the mind in evaluating, testing and making a judgement. It is an ability that is sensitized and developed as we grow in the Lord and renew our minds in His word according to the admonition in Romans 12:2.

An important verse concerning "thinking critically" is 1 Corinthians 14:29, where Paul says, "Let two or three prophets speak, and let the others judge." The "others" in this passage would be the "others" in the Christian assembly, which in Paul's day met primarily in homes.

It should also be noted that Paul is not here referring to an elite company of "prophets" in the Corinthian congregation. The noun "prophets" is functional language and refers to anyone in the congregation who is moved to speak a word of prophecy. "Prophet" is here used in the same way as "interpreter" is used in vs. 28.

Verse 31 makes it clear that all have the potential to prophesy. In the same way that all have the potential to prophesy, all are expected to "judge" the prophecies that come forth.

The word "judge" is from the Greek word *diakrino*, and although it is variously translated as "judge," "discern" and "weigh carefully," the word literally means "to separate" or "to discriminate."

In other words, we are to sit in judgment and separate truth from error. With sanctified common sense, a heart yielded to the Holy Spirit, and the word of God as our guide, we are to evaluate and make judgments concerning things both natural and spiritual. This is what it means to "think critically" and it is the responsibility of the entire body of Christ.

We Will Judge Angels

As a young Christian with limited finances, I made an emotional commitment to give a certain offering to an evangelist. Afterwards, I regretted the decision because of questionable tactics in his ministry. This created a tension in my heart because I also felt that I had obligated myself by receiving his offering envelope.

As I went to prayer asking the Lord what I should do, I heard Him say, "Do whatever you think is best." I knew at that moment that God was leaving the judgment and decision with me and would be OK with whatever I decided. I reached over, picked up the offering envelope I had taken and threw it in the garbage. It was a very liberating moment.

I then read where Paul, in I Corinthians 6:1-6, admonished the Corinthians for taking their disputes before pagan judges, and not judging the issues themselves. He exhorted them that even the "least esteemed" among them were able to make judgements concerning their disagreements. He exclaimed,

> *Do you not know that the saints shall judge the world? And if the world will be judged by you are you unworthy to judge the smallest matters? Do you not know that we shall judge angels? How much more things that pertain to this life?*

Concluding Thought

You never have to fear when it comes to "thinking critically." God will never reprimand us for doing what He has commanded us to do. He has commanded us to "think critically" and to "test the spirits." If we do it in integrity and to the best of our ability, God will not judge us even if we miss it.

Many tragedies in Christian history could have been avoided if the people had been taught to "think critically."

Always remember, both Scripture and history teach us that the perils of not thinking critically are far greater than the perils of being mistaken a time or two in our evaluations and judgments.

Chapter 8

John Wesley Shows How to Test the Spirits

"Try all things by the written word and let all bow down before it."
John Wesley

The eighteenth-century Methodist Revival emerged as one of the most powerful and enduring revivals of Christian history. John Wesley's emphasis on Biblical truth coupled with his openness to the dynamic working of the Holy Spirit gave the revival a unique stability, resulting in much good fruit, not only in the first generation, but in succeeding generations. This is why the noted historian, Dr. Vinson Synan, has called John Wesley "The Father," not only of Methodism, but of all the Holiness-Pentecostal bodies that have emerged from it.

The Bible Was Their Guide

The revival began with John Wesley, his brother Charles, and several of their colleagues at Oxford University meeting together each evening from 6 to 9 p.m. to study the Greek New Testament. They were members of the Church of England (Anglican) but were dubbed Methodists for their methodical approach to Biblical study and other Christian disciplines.

They were people of the Word who made the Bible their ultimate guide for life and faith. In 1729 John Wesley, who taught Greek and logical thinking at Oxford, wrote,

I began to not only read, but to study the Bible as
the one and the only standard of truth, and the
only model of pure religion.[14]

George Whitefield, an early colleague of the Wesleys, and
revivalist extraordinaire, also exhibited a great hunger for
Biblical truth. Shortly after meeting Charles Wesley at
Oxford, he had a dramatic born-again experience and was
consumed with a hunger for God's word. He wrote,

My mind now being more open and enlarged, I
began to read the Holy Scriptures upon my knees,
laying aside all other books and praying over, if
possible, every line and word.[15]

Revival Birthed in Prayer

John Wesley and the early Methodists did not seek an
experience, or an event, called "revival." They sought a
restoration of what they called "primitive Christianity."
In this quest to discover the Christianity of the New
Testament, they not only diligently studied the
Scriptures, they also prayed. In fact, the Methodist
revival can, perhaps, be traced to an all-night prayer
meeting that began on December 31, 1738.

About seventy Methodists, many of them Anglican
ministers, as were John and Charles, gathered on New
Year's Eve for a night of prayer. It proved to be a very

---

14 John Wesley, *A Plain Account of Christian Perfection*
(London: Epworth, 1952), 6.

15 George Whitefield, *George Whitefield's Journals* (Carlisle, PA:
Banner of Truth Trust, 1960), 60.

eventful time. The next day, January 1, 1739, John Wesley recorded in his *Journal*:

> At about three in the morning, as we were continuing instant in prayer, the power of God came mightily upon us insomuch that many cried out for exceeding joy, and many fell to the ground. We broke out with one voice, "We praise thee, O God, we acknowledge thee to be the Lord."[16]

Shut out of the Anglican churches with whom they were ordained, Wesley, Whitefield and others began to preach on the streets and in open fields. Thousands came out to hear them preach, and British society was transformed as God's Spirit was poured out through them.

In the midst of this revival many dramatic and often bizarre manifestations occurred, including falling, shaking, weeping, shouting, visions and trances. Wesley's *Journal* describes a remarkable scene that occurred in the Anglican church in Everton as God's Spirit was poured out and the people were overwhelmed with the convicting power of God's presence. An eyewitness wrote,

> This occasioned a mixture of various sounds; some shrieking, some roaring aloud. The most general was a loud breathing, like that of people half strangled and gasping for life. Great numbers wept without any noise; others fell down as dead; some sinking in silence; some with extreme noise

---

[16] Eddie Hyatt, *2000 Years of Charismatic Christianity* (Lake Mary, FL: Charisma House, 2002), 102.

and violent agitation.[11]

He Sees the Need to Discern & Judge

As the revival progressed, Wesley realized that there was a mixture and a need to discern between the true and the false. In his *Journal*, he says that "nature mixed with grace" as some sought to imitate the cries and convulsions of those who had been truly overwhelmed by the Spirit. He also admitted that demonically inspired manifestations appeared, saying, "Satan likewise mimicked this work of God, in order to discredit the whole work."[17]

One of Wesley's most powerful preachers, George Bell, began to think of himself as a prophet and to think that every strong impression on his mind was a revelation from God. This led to many bizarre declarations, including a prophecy that the world would end on February 28, 1763.

Wesley sought to reason with Bell, but he had become full of himself and would not hear correction. Wesley finally excommunicated him, and exhorted the people,

> Try all things by the written word and let all bow down before it. You're in danger of enthusiasm every hour, if you depart ever so little from the Scripture: yea; from that plain, literal meaning of any text, taken with the context.

Dreams and visions abounded in the Methodist revival and Wesley found a need to discriminate between those

---

[17] John Wesley, vol. 8 of *The Works of John Wesley*, 14 vols. (Grand Rapids: Zondervan, n.d.), 519.

that were real and those that were the product of an over-active imagination. His colleague and biographer, Thomas Coke, wrote of this problem, saying that Wesley found it necessary to confront some who gave undue attention "to dreams, visions and man's own imaginations and feelings, without bringing them to the only true test, the oracles of God."[18]

One such confrontation took place at the Methodist society at the Fish-Ponds. Wesley said he went to the meeting full of the thought from I John 4:1, *Beloved, believe not every spirit, but try the spirits whether they are of God*. He later recorded in his *Journal*,

> I told them they were not to judge the spirit whereby anyone spoke, either by appearances, or by common report, or by their own inward feelings: No, nor by dreams, visions, or revelations, supposed to be made to their souls; any more than by their tears, or any involuntary effects wrought upon their bodies. I warned them that all these were, in themselves, of a doubtful, disputable, nature; they might be from God, and they might not; and were therefore not simply to be relied on (any more than to be simply condemned) but to be tried by a farther rule, to be brought to the only certain test, the Law and the Testimony.

The "Law and the Testimony" is a reference to the Scriptures found in Isaiah 8:20. Wesley was a stickler for the Word.

---

18 Dr. Coke and Mr. Moore, *Life of the Rev. John Wesley, A.M.* (Philadelphia: Printed by Parry Hall, MDCCXCII), 157.

Scripture was to be the final guide and authority in all questionable matters. He also emphasized "common sense," which he called "reason," as a secondary guide in all spiritual matters.

These guides were obvious in a conversation he had with another group of Methodists who told him they had experienced the blood of Christ running up their arms, or going down their throat, or pounding like warm water upon their chest and heart. Wesley said,

> I plainly told them the utmost I could allow, without renouncing both **Scripture and reason**, was that some of these circumstances might be from God (though I could not affirm they were) working in an unusual manner, no way essential to either justification or sanctification; but that all the rest I must believe to be the mere empty dreams of a heated imagination.[19]

Don't Try to Make the "Unusual" the "Norm"

Wesley wisely judged between the "unusual" and the "norm" of Christianity. He recognized that when God visits a people in great power, there will be, especially in the beginning, unusual manifestations that were never meant to be the "norm" of the Christian life.

Paul experienced this in Ephesus where Luke says that God worked *unusual miracles* through the hands of Paul (Acts 19:11). This is when handkerchiefs and aprons were

---

[19] Wesley, vol. 1, 426-27, Sept. 6, 1742.

taken from Paul's body and then laid on the sick and demon possessed. As a result, miracles of healing and deliverance occurred.

Paul, however, recognized that this was not the norm and he never mentioned this incident in any of his letters. Nor did Luke mention it as ever occurring again in Paul's ministry. It was something God did especially for the situation in Ephesus and Paul knew it was not to become a formula, method or norm of ministry.

When my father was baptized in the Holy Spirit during a time of revival around 1940, he was so overwhelmed by the Holy Spirit that he could not speak in English for several hours. Even after leaving the meeting, he would speak to my mother and it would come out in tongues.

In my Dad's later years, I asked him if he ever had that sort of experience again. He replied, "No, that was the only time." Even though my Dad's experience was genuine, it would have been wrong for him to try and make that experience the norm for himself and others.

Some contemporary revivalists have tried to make Paul's visit to the third heaven a "norm." Paul, however, only mentions such an experience once, and at the time of mention, it had happened fourteen years before (II Corinthians 12:2). It is, therefore, foolish and dangerous to try and make Paul's one time experience the norm for believers today. It was not even the norm for Paul.

Wesley came to realize that dramatic and violent manifestations such as shaking, falling and convulsing were not the Biblical norm and should not be pursued. Later in life, he wrote,

I have generally observed more or less of these outward symptoms (falling, shaking, convulsing, shouting, etc.) to attend the beginning of a general work of God: So it was in New England, Scotland, Holland, Ireland, and many parts of England; but after a time they gradually decrease, and the work goes on more quietly and silently. Those whom it pleases God to employ in His work, ought to be quite passive in this respect: They should choose nothing but leave entirely to him all the circumstances of his own work.[20]

The concern to acknowledge true manifestations but not make them objects of pursuit was shared by other Methodist leaders. This is the basis on which Whitefield wrote a letter to Wesley, dated June 25, 1739, in which he exhorted Wesley to neither require nor encourage such manifestations. He wrote,

I think it is tempting God to require such signs. That there is something of God in it, I doubt not. But the devil, I believe, does interpose. I think it will encourage the French Prophets, take people away from the written word, and make them depend on visions, convulsions, etc., more than on the promises and precepts of the gospel.[21]

Wesley's Balanced Approach

Wesley's attitude toward unusual spiritual manifestations may be described as "being open without

---

[20] Wesley, vol. 2 of *The Works of John Wesley*, 510.

[21] Whitfield, 497.

being naïve and being critical without being judgmental." He gave neither a blanket endorsement nor a blanket condemnation to such manifestations but judged each one individually on its own merits; the bottom line being that manifestations are not to be sought for their own value.

This approach of judging each spiritual manifestation on its own merits is important for there can be similar manifestations but with different origins. For example, in the 1990s this writer visited a well-known center of revival where manifestations such as falling, shouting, shaking and laughing were occurring, and I came away with a deep sense of peace and refreshing.

Not long, thereafter, I visited another "revival" where the same sort of manifestations were occurring. I left that meeting so deeply grieved in my spirit. There was a rank spiritual odor about the whole affair, so much so that my response was, "If this is revival I want nothing to do with it."

In the first instance, there was a genuine work of the Holy Spirit. In the second, I suspect that someone—perhaps the leaders—had visited a genuine revival somewhere and came home determined that they too would have a revival. Sadly, they equated the manifestations with revival and were, therefore, seeking manifestations. They were not seeking God.

Theirs was a fleshly or soulish revival that had been worked up and not prayed down. Their version of "revival" was described by R. A. Torrey, an associate of

D. L. Moody and a successful revivalist in his own right. He wrote,

> We frequently have religious excitements and enthusiasms gotten up by the cunning methods and hypnotic influence of the mere professional evangelist or "revivalist," but these are not Revivals, and are not needed: they are a curse and not a blessing; they are the devil's imitations of a Revival.[22]

A Model for This Generation

Wesley was very honest in evaluating the state of the revival he spearheaded and led for fifty years. About twenty years into the revival, he wrote,

> At first, it was doubtless wholly from God. It is partly so at this day; and He will enable us to discern how far, in every case, the work is pure, and where it mixes and degenerates.[23]

Because of Wesley's honest commitment to lead and pastor the revival, it maintained a level of purity as it spread throughout the United Kingdom and transformed British society. It was then brought to America where Methodist circuit riding preachers played an important role in taming the rugged American frontier and in igniting the Second Great Awakening.

---

[22] R. A. Torrey, *The Power of Prayer and the Prayer of Power* (Grand Rapids: Zondervan, 1924), 228.

[23] Wesley, vol. 8 of *The Works of John Wesley*, 519.

Wesley's openness to the dynamic working of the Holy balanced by a commitment to the Scriptures and a down-to-earth common sense is a model that this generation of Christian leaders would be wise to follow.

Chapter 9

Charismatic Credulity
Lessons from an Old Smelly Sock

"They felt no need to lie on the slab from which He had risen or stand on the spot from which He had ascended. Collecting relics and establishing shrines never entered their thinking. Christ Himself was living in them and everything else paled in comparison to that wonderful reality."

Eddie L. Hyatt

"What is she doing with that old sock under her pillow," exclaimed the pastor to his mother who was making the beds and had just found one of my socks under the pillow of his seventeen-year-old sister. I was a young, single preacher at the time and had preached in this church several times; and each time I stayed in the home of the pastor who lived with his parents and four siblings.

His younger sister apparently developed a crush on me and found a sock I left behind, which she then arranged under her pillow. During a return visit, the pastor's mother, with a chuckle, told me about finding the sock, and her son's (the pastor's) amazement that his sister would be sleeping with an "old sock" under her pillow.

Sue is Not Enamored with My Socks

Now, Sue does not sleep with my socks under her pillow. She is not impressed with my socks. In fact, she will chide me if I leave them lying around. Why is Sue not enamored with my socks? She has me! Because the young lady mentioned above did not have me, my sock was very important to her.

The Disciples Were Not Enamored with Jesus' Socks

Do you realize that the disciples never carried Jesus' socks or any of His clothing around with them? Think about it! There is absolutely no evidence that the disciples tried to preserve Jesus' grave clothes, nor any of his clothes or possessions. They never chipped any rocks off the stone where He lay and from which He was resurrected and sent them out for love offerings. (I am being a little fastidious here).

Why did they have no interest in His clothes or possessions? It was because they had Jesus Himself. They knew He was alive, and by His Spirit, was living in them. Why would they have any interest in His socks, or any part of His clothing, when He Himself was with them? It was not a mere doctrine, it was a living reality!

It was for this same reason that they never held special impartation services at the tomb or on the Mt. Olives from which Jesus had ascended into heaven. They never tried to preserve pieces of the cross and they never encouraged believers to make a pilgrimage to Jerusalem. Why? Because they knew He was alive and was living with them and in them.

Socks Took the Place of the Real Presence of Jesus

It was only after several generations, when the church had lost the knowledge and awareness of His real abiding presence, that emphases began to be put on His clothing, pieces of the cross, and the bones and relics of the saints.

When the crusaders returned to western Europe from Jerusalem they (supposedly) brought with them Christ's seamless garment, the iron head of the spear that pierced his side, the cross, multiple pieces from the cross, straw from the manger, John the Baptist's head, vials of milk from the virgin Mary, the finger that Thomas thrust into the side of Jesus, and countless other bones and relics from the early saints. These were publicly paraded with great fanfare, with claims of miracles, including the raising of the dead, everywhere they were taken.

Defenders of such superstitious activity pointed to Paul in Ephesus and the handkerchiefs and aprons that were taken from him and placed on the sick and diseased (Acts 19:11-12). As mentioned in the previous chapter, however, this was an isolated incident recorded by Luke and Paul never mentions it (or anything similar) in all his letters. It was obviously something he did not want to perpetuate.

It is also obvious from Luke's account that the initiative for taking these handkerchiefs and aprons (normal apparel in the ancient world) did not lie with Paul but with others. Can you imagine Paul sending out pieces of his clothing or a prayer cloth in return for a love offering? I can't! His revelation of the reality of Christ living in and through God's people left no room for such self-serving credulity.

Pentecostals Have Not Been Free
From Such Superstition

I grew up in a Pentecostal pastor's home during the time of the famed healing revival of the 1950s. I recall as a child attending the giant tents of the healing evangelists. I remember claims of bloody crosses appearing on people, sometimes in the forehead and sometimes in the palm of the hand. There were frightening prophecies of the end of the world and that this revival was God's final call before the return of Christ. There were also claims of miracle oil, miracle billfolds (that would never be empty of money), miracle cloths, blessing kits, and all sorts of gimmicks that could be obtained for a love offering to the evangelist.

There was one well-known pastor/evangelist in our area who had a miracle chair in which he would have people to sit who needed a miracle. He also gave out prayer cloths that were color coded for different kinds of demons and sicknesses. He also had a red string for those to wear who needed to lose weight.

A cousin went to him and was miraculously healed of terminal cancer. Her hometown newspaper did a full-page write up with photos about the healing. The cancer, however, later returned and she died.

The miracle chair and the colored cloths would not work their magic the second time around. If she had known the reality of Christ within and the faithfulness of His word, she could have been healed through faith in Him and not have fallen prey to such credulity.

Holy Ghost Feathers

Because many charismatics are so eager to see miracles, it makes them vulnerable to deception. For example, in the 1990s at a large Christian gathering in Tulsa, feathers suddenly appeared, floating all over the platform. This happened while the featured speaker, known as Sister Lucy, was praying for another well-known woman minister.

Sister Lucy made a big deal about it, whipping the crowd into feverish shouts of praise as she proclaimed that these were "Holy Ghost feathers." Many, including well-known ministers, were taken in by this exotic manifestation and the surrounding hype.

However, a local pastor, Willie George, was willing to "think critically" about it all. He obtained a video of the meeting and discovered it was all a farce. He then produced a video from the original footage and showed, by slowing down the video at the right places, that she had released the feathers from the sleeve of her top.

This woman also claimed to experience the wounds of Jesus in her hands, forehead and back. She also claimed to experience miracle oil flowing from her hands. She was discredited, however, and left town. I had not heard of her in years until I was recently in Toronto, Canada and was told that she was ministering at a large charismatic church in that city.

Superstition in the Contemporary Charismatic Movement

Yes, charismatic credulity is alive and well in the charismatic revival movement today. A pastor friend shared with me about an acquaintance of his who located A. A. Allen's grave in Miracle Valley, AZ and went and lay on the grave for several hours hoping to "soak up" some of the anointing from Allen's bones. Another person lay for hours on the grave of John G. Lake hoping for similar results.

Parallel with this is the popular idea that certain geographic locations hold some sort of special anointing that can be tapped into and that this anointing can be carried around and imparted to others. This sort of thinking has also opened the door to credulous, unbiblical thinking about receiving the mantles of past revivalists and about angels who supposedly hold sway over different areas of geography, commerce, healing, revival, etc. This is medieval superstition rearing its head in the current revival movement and it is leading people away from the knowledge of Christ Himself.

Know Who You Are

The early disciples of Jesus never did this sort of thing. They were not interested in Jesus' socks or any part of his clothing. They felt no need to lie on the slab from which He had risen or stand on the spot from which He had ascended. Collecting relics and establishing shrines never entered their thinking. Christ Himself was living in them and everything else paled in comparison to that wonderful reality.

Paul expresses this amazing truth using the Greek word *naos*, which is often translated as "temple.' In his first letter to the Corinthians, Paul chides them for not knowing who they are and then telling them that they, both corporately and individually, are the *naos* (temple) of God" (I Corinthians 3:16; 6:19).

There was another Greek word for "temple" that Paul could have used—the word *heron*. *Heron* referred to the entire temple complex with all its porches, courts, rooms, gates, etc. The word Paul used, *naos*, referred specifically to the innermost sanctuary—the Holy of Holies—where God's presence dwelt and His shekinah glory was manifest.

Paul use of *naos* is, therefore, of great significance. He tells the Corinthian believers that they are now God's dwelling place. They are now the Holy of Holies. They themselves are God's *hagios naos*—His holy sanctuary.

No wonder the earliest Christians had no interest in religious fetishes and icons! They lived in the reality that they themselves were God's dwelling place. They knew the reality of I John 4:4, *Greater is He that is in you, than he that is in the world*. Angels, miracles and all other spiritual phenomena paled alongside this wonderful reality.

This also means that we are not "ushered into the presence of God" by stirring music and a hyped atmosphere. That is soulish. You, as God's child, are His *naos*. You are His sanctuary. He lives in you and that is a factual reality regardless of where you are and how you feel.

This means you do not have to travel to Tulsa, Toronto, Redding, Rome or any other place to have an encounter with Him. Right where you are, you can know and experience the most wonderful reality in all the universe—Christ in you the hope of glory (Col. 1:26). Anything less is nothing but an old smelly sock.

Chapter 10

Loving Truth:
The Antidote for Deception

*The coming of the lawless one will be in accordance with the work of Satan displayed in all kinds of counterfeit miracles, signs and wonders, and in every sort of evil that deceives those who are perishing. **They perish because they refused to love the truth**.*

II Thess. 2:9-10; NIV

Is it possible that "Spirit-filled" Christians are opening the door to lying and deceptive spirits by their reckless handling of the truth? Consider the following facts.

- A Christian leader, whose book had just been pulled because the publisher discovered that his testimony of being delivered from Satanism was greatly exaggerated, defended his actions, saying that it is OK to "embellish" one's story to make the gospel more attractive.

- Shortly after 911 a well-known "prophet" declared on national TV that Bin Laden would be found within thirty-five days. When, months later, he was confronted by the fact that it did not happen, he sought to justify himself saying that he had not stated what point the thirty-five days was from.

- A TV evangelist, who was discovered using an earpiece to receive "words of knowledge" from his wife about people in the audience, justified his actions saying it built people's faith and helped them receive from God.

- In a recent high profile "revival" it was reported that over thirty people had been raised from the dead, but when Christian journalists sought to interview some of them, not a single one could be found.

- A well-known pastor and worship leader received both sympathy and money while faking terminal cancer for two years, even appearing in concert with an oxygen tank and a tube in his nose before finally confessing it was all a hoax.

And the list goes on.

A Cavalier Approach to Truth Opens the Door to Deception

Such cavalier handling of truth seems to be rampant in charismatic circles. Such behavior, however, is spiritually dangerous. Both Old and New Testaments reveal that "fudging" or compromising truth opens one to lying and deceptive spirits. In speaking of the rampant deception that will be characteristic of the last days, Paul, in II Thess. 2:9-11, says that those who are deceived will perish *because they refused to love the truth* (NIV). Those who do not love the truth find themselves defenseless against the "father of lies" (Jn. 8:44).

An Old Testament Example

This principle is clearly borne out in the Old Testament account of four hundred prophets being deceived by a lying spirit because they were willing to "fudge" the truth for personal gain.

In I Kings 22, Ahab, the wicked king of Israel, asks Jehoshaphat, the righteous king of Judah, to go to battle with him against the Syrians. Jehoshaphat agrees but suggests that they first inquire of the Lord through the prophets concerning the matter. Ahab agrees and sends for his four hundred court prophets who are probably products of the "school of the prophets," often referred to in the Old Testament as the "sons of the prophets" or the "company of prophets."

Politicized Prophets

We are not told how the "school of the prophets" began and Scripture neither affirms nor condemns the school. Some believe it was begun by Samuel to prepare young men for prophetic ministry. Nonetheless, it is clear, that through the "school of the prophets," prophetic ministry was professionalized and became a vocation by which the prophet made his living. Some were hired by the wealthy and kings kept many in their courts as advisers and to inquire of them concerning the mind of the Lord.

As a result, prophetic ministry became politicized with many of these "prophets" yielding to the pressure to prophesy that which would please those in power, from whom they also received their livelihood. Their willingness to compromise truth opened them to lying spirits.

At Ahab's command, these four hundred "school of the prophets" graduates come before the two kings. They all declared the same message. The two kings are to go out against the Syrians and God will give them a great victory.

There is even a prophetic drama as one of the prophets, Zedekiah, takes horns of iron and declares, *Thus says the LORD with these you shall gore the Syrians until they are destroyed* (22:11).

A Prophet Who Will
Not Compromise Truth

Jehoshaphat apparently does not feel settled with what he is hearing and asks Ahab if there was not another prophet from whom they could inquire. Ahab sullenly replies that there is one more by the name of Micaiah, *but I hate him because he does not prophesy good concerning me, but evil* (22:8). Ah, here is a prophet who is committed to truth and will not compromise even when it offends the king. He is no political prophet. He is not trying to impress anyone. He is committed to truth.

At Jehoshaphat's insistence, Ahab calls for Micaiah. The messenger who goes for Micaiah informs him that the four hundred prophets are all in agreement and exhorts him to let his word agree with theirs, *i.e.*, to get in unity with the other prophets. Micaiah replies that he will speak whatever word the Lord may give him.

We must remember that our ultimate goal is not unity, but conformity to Christ who is Truth personified. True Biblical unity is always built on truth.

A Lying Spirit Released into
The Mouths of the Prophets

Micaiah arrives and after a brief exchange with Ahab relates an astounding vision he has seen. Micaiah says he saw the Lord sitting on His throne and all the host of heaven standing by. He heard the Lord say, *Who will persuade Ahab to go up, that he may fall [die] at Ramoth Gilead* (22:20). Different ones offered suggestions, but then a spirit came and stood before the Lord and said, ***I will go and be a lying spirit in the mouth of all his prophets*** (22:22). Micaiah then heard the Lord say to the spirit, *You shall persuade him and also prevail. Go and do so* (22:22). Micaiah then declared to Ahab, *Therefore look! The Lord has put a lying spirit in the mouth of all these prophets of yours, and the Lord has declared disaster against you* (22:23).

Ahab responded in anger, ordering Micaiah to be imprisoned and fed only bread and water. The other prophets were also offended and one of them, Zedekiah, *went up and slapped Micaiah in the face* (22:24). Ahab and Jehoshaphat chose to ignore Micaiah's word and proceeded into battle where Ahab was killed, and the armies of Israel and Judah were forced to withdraw, just as Micaiah had predicted.

How did a lying spirit find its way into the mouths of these prophets who prophesied in the name of the God of Israel? There is no question that their willingness to fudge the truth for personal and political gain opened the door. It still happens today.

It Still Happens Today

I remember a Christian leader, whom I respect, tell about attending a meeting where the evangelist was, reportedly, functioning in the gifts of the Spirit in a remarkable way, particularly in prophecy and the word of knowledge. He said the man ministered in an entertaining sort of way revealing personal things about people in the congregation, even telling one man the brand of cigarettes he had hidden in his pocket.

While observing this, Kenneth E. Hagin said he heard a voice say, "familiar spirit." The voice was so clear that he instinctively looked around to see if someone next to him had spoken. He then realized it was the Holy Spirit speaking in his heart that this was a familiar spirit at work.

Knowing something of the man's background and ministry, he realized that the man had built his ministry, not on the word of God and truth, but on the sensational gifts of the Spirit. When the gift was not operating by the Spirit, (I Cor. 12:11), this man, to draw the crowds, had sought to operate the gift out of his own soul. This involved being less than honest; and by playing fast and loose with the truth he had opened himself to a familiar/lying spirit.

Closing the Door on Satan

There has been so much reckless twisting of truth and so much gullibility in charismatic circles that I have wondered if some may not be among the first to embrace the anti-Christ when he comes on the scene. Deception gives birth to more deception. Speaking of the great deception of the last days, Paul tells the consequences for those who refuse to love the truth. He says,

> *For this reason [not loving truth] God sends them a powerful delusion so that they will believe the lie, and so that all will be condemned who have not believed the truth but have delighted in wickedness* (II Thess. 2:11-12; NIV).

We can close the door on lying and deceptive spirits by loving truth. Satan traffics in lies and deceptions, for this is his only means of power and control. This is why Jesus said in Jn. 8:31-32, *If you continue in My word, you are my disciples indeed; and you shall know the truth and the truth shall make you free.* When we love and walk in truth, there is no place for Satan in our lives.

Hear the words of Paul in II Cor. 4:2-5 concerning his commitment to integrity and truth. This statement is a wonderful guide that we should all utilize. What a difference it would make in the body of Christ today. Paul says,

> *We have renounced secret and shameful ways; we do not use deception, nor do we distort the word of God. On the contrary, by setting forth the truth plainly we commend ourselves to every man's conscience in the sight of God . . . For we do not preach ourselves, but Jesus Christ as Lord, and ourselves as your servants for Jesus' sake* (NIV).

Chapter 11

The Colossian Heresy Revisited

Do not let anyone disqualify you, insisting on self-abasement and worship of angels, dwelling on visions, puffed up without cause by a human way of thinking.

Colossians 2:18 (NRSV)

While driving to class one day, I asked God for a theme for the class I would be teaching from Paul's letter to Colosse. As I prayed, the phrase "Don't Lose Your Focus" was strongly impressed upon my heart and mind. This phrase remained in my heart as I prayed and worshipped during the 25-minute drive to the campus.

At the beginning of the class, I wrote across the board in large letters "DON'T LOSE YOUR FOCUS" and announced it as the theme, even though I had no idea how it would apply. I was then astounded at the sequence of events that unfolded.

As I taught that morning, the Holy Spirit directed our attention to what New Testament scholars call "The Colossian Heresy." Although I had taught on the subject before, on this particular day new and fresh insight unfolded into the nature of this first century heresy. In essence, they had lost their focus on Christ, being distracted by other, even legitimate, things.

After the class was over I went to a nearby auditorium to hear a well-known guest speaker. As I listened to this individual, who is well known in the revival/prophetic movement, I was astounded to hear the Colossian Heresy that I had just delineated being propagated all over again.

The Colossians Had Lost Their Focus

What was it that was distracting the Colossians and causing them to lose their focus? They had become obsessed with how to be "spiritual" and had become enamored with supernatural phenomena such as visions and angelic visitations (2:18). The Colossian Heresy was, in essence, an unhealthy preoccupation on the part of the Colossian believers with their own spirituality, which they based on the number of angels and visions they had seen.

Paul's answer was to direct their attention back to Christ as the source and fullness of everything they needed. They did not need to look to angels or any other source for knowledge of God, *For in Him [Christ] dwells all the fullness of the Godhead bodily* (2:9). There was no need to look elsewhere for salvation and healing for, *You are complete in Him who is the Head of all principality and power* (2:10). They did not need to turn to other avenues for obtaining special wisdom and knowledge, for in Christ, *Are hidden all the treasures of wisdom and knowledge* (2:3).

A Religious Fascination With Angels & Visions

In 2:18 Paul chides the Colossians for *the worship of angels* and for *dwelling on visions* (NRSV). The word "worship" in this passage is a translation of the Greek word *threskia* and is not the normal word for "worship." Besides Col. 2:18 it is found in only three other places in the New Testament, Acts 26:3 and James 1:26, 27, where it is translated as "religion."

The point seems to be that the Colossians had developed a "religious fascination" with angels and visions.

Because of their fascination with such esoteric, sensational phenomena, they are no longer, *Holding fast to the Head from whom all the body, nourished and knit together . . . grows with an increase that is from God* (2:19). This is serious, for only by abiding in Christ and holding fast to Him can the Colossians experience the fullness of salvation and arrive at spiritual maturity.

Spiritual Pride Intrudes

To complicate matters, the spiritual experiences, with which they are so enamored, have become a basis for pride. They consider themselves a notch above other Christians because of their spiritual experiences. They are an elite group. Although they purport to be humble, it is a false humility that is betrayed by their attitudes and actions (2:18). Perhaps referring to their most prominent teacher, Paul says that he, like his followers, is *vainly puffed up by his fleshly mind* (2:18).

The Colossian Heresy Today

As I sat and listened to this guest speaker, I was amazed at how closely their message coincided with the Colossian Heresy the Holy Spirit had just delineated for us. Their message seemed to be all about angels, visions and prophecy with little or no mention of Jesus.

I suddenly realized that the Colossian Heresy was being unwittingly propagated again under the guise of "revival" and the "prophetic." I somberly realized that those, including myself, who long for genuine Spiritual awakenings must guard against an unhealthy preoccupation with sensational phenomena lest we too lose our focus on Jesus and, thereby, repeat "The Colossian Heresy."

Suggestions for not Repeating The Colossian Heresy

1) Keep Jesus front and center. Hold fast (cling) to the Head (Jesus) *from whom all the body is nourished and knit together* (Colossians 2:19).

2) Stop seeking spiritual experiences. *Seek the Lord and you shall live* (Amos 5:5). We are not to follow signs, signs are to follow us as we seek and obey Him (Mark 16:17).

3) Build your life and ministry on the word of God. Remember that Jesus overcame Satan by saying, "It is written," not by recounting the voice from heaven, prophecies, or angelic visitations.

4) Let the supernatural happen; don't try to make it happen. When Christians try to make the supernatural happen, they inevitably get in the flesh and open themselves to "angels of light" who prey on the naive and the prideful.

5) Stay humble. Avoid an elitist attitude. Remember that "pride is the stronghold of deception."

Chapter 12

5 Reasons I Do Not Practice Contemplative Prayer

"It is striking how rarely Christ appeared in all these "revelations," "apparitions," and "wonders." Catholics who followed in the wake of every new revelation . . . who had never once in their whole lives read the Scriptures from cover to cover."

Dr. Hans Kung, Catholic Theologian

I value quietness and solitude. In fact, it was during such a time that I received inspiration and direction for this chapter. One morning I found myself wide awake at 3 a.m. Not wanting to keep Sue awake, I went to another room and sat in a chair, where in the stillness and quietness, I thought about God and His goodness and faithfulness.

At times I would voice quiet words of praise and thanksgiving as I thought on His majesty and greatness. As needs and concerns came to mind, I would present these in prayer. It was a wonderful, refreshing time: And somewhere, during those quiet hours of fellowship with God, the title and layout for this chapter were presented to my mind.

My Experience with Contemplative Prayer

Contemplative prayer is commonly associated with words and phrases such as "spiritual formation," "silence," "centering prayer," and "mysticism." I first became acquainted with contemplative prayer through in-depth studies of church history, particularly of monastic and mystical movements during the Middle Ages.

I have also become acquainted through personal experience. As part of a doctoral course, my wife, Susan, and I attended a retreat that used the contemplative, mystical model. We were required to take a vow of silence and there was much talk about the monastic "desert fathers." I came away with a deep sense that this was a subtle substitute for the authentic spirituality of the New Testament.

Here are five reasons I do not practice contemplative prayer.

Reason #1
Contemplative Prayer is Rooted
In a non-Christian Concept of God

Contemplative prayer is rooted in a pagan idea of a supreme being who is impassible, *i.e.,* one who is unmoved by human experiences of joy, sadness, or suffering. This is because he is absolutely "other than" and "separate from" this realm of physical and human existence.

The ancient Greeks—particularly the Neoplatonists and the Gnostics--theorized that from this one supreme being had issued forth a series of lower beings resulting in a hierarchy of celestial beings. They believed that it was one of these lower (and evil) beings, Yahweh of the Old Testament, that had created the earth and its inhabitants. The Neoplatonists sought for a way to ascend through this hierarchy of celestial beings and be united with the ultimate god whom they called "the One."

Because "the One" existed in a realm absolutely "other than" this earthly realm, human reason and language were deemed inadequate for understanding or communicating with him. In fact, "the One" could not be known by human beings, but could only be experienced in a mystical encounter facilitated by a form of spiritual prayer characterized by silence and a mind emptied of any rational thoughts about deity. If one was unable to clear his/her mind of debilitating thoughts, a "mantra" or "prayer" might be repeated over and over to help them center their thoughts on the task at hand—a mystical union with "the One."

This concept of God and the form of contemplative prayer associated with it, found its way into the church of the Middle Ages, particularly through the writings of a Syrian monk who was obviously profoundly influenced by Neoplatonism. The writings of this monk, who falsely claimed to be Dyonisius, Paul's convert in Athens, became foundational for the mystical movement in the medieval church.

This false Dyonisius was quoted by bishops and some of the most famous theologians of the medieval church, including Thomas Aquinas. As a result, spiritual experiences and revelations through contemplation were exalted and valued while the Scriptures were often ignored, and at times, even banned by the institutional church. Exotic, non-Biblical miracles such as levitations, communion wafers bleeding, statues weeping, apparitions of the saints and the Virgin Mary, etc. were hailed as the great works of God.

This is not to say that the mystics were bad people, but it is to say that they unwittingly embraced non-Christian concepts of God and prayer, and that is why I do not practice contemplative prayer.

Reason #2
Contemplative Prayer Erroneously Assumes that Words and Rational Thoughts are Useless When it Comes to Prayer

Contemplative prayer is prayer without thought and words. It is rooted in the pagan idea that human thought and language is inadequate for communicating with a transcendent divine being. One must, therefore, find God in silence; or, as one mystic put it, "in the quiet dark in which all who love God lose themselves."

For those committed to this approach, it is forms, techniques, and postures of prayer and meditation that are important, for these help facilitate the contemplation and silence that will lead to an encounter or union with God. One striking example is that of Gregory Palamas, a thirteenth century monk who stressed quietness and stillness in the pursuit of a mystical union with God. As an aid to concentration, he recommended that the chin rest on the chest, with the eyes fixed on the navel.

The God of the Bible is so different from this contemplative approach. There is no demeaning of human thought and language as a means of communicating with God. In the Old Testament, God communicates His message again and again to the people in their language through the prophets. It is obvious that He expects the people to communicate with Him in their own language. Through the prophet Isaiah He invites his unfaithful people to, *Come now and let us reason together*.

It is obvious that He wants the people to know Him in a real and personal way, and not just have some esoteric, mystical encounter with Him. Through the prophet Jeremiah He declared,

> *Let not the wise man boast of his wisdom or the strong man boast of his strength . . . but let him who boasts boast about this that he understands and knows me, that I am the LORD, who exercises kindness, justice and righteousness on earth, for in these I delight.*

This truth comes through in an even more pronounced way in the New Testament. For both Jesus and His earliest followers, prayer is about open communication with God in one's own tongue. Through the baptism in the Holy Spirit the prayer life of the New Testament believer is enhanced, not through silence, but through greater dimensions of speech, *i.e.,* praying in tongues.

Of course, neither Jesus nor Paul advocated the rejection of the intellect or rational thinking. In fact, Jesus said that we are to love God with all our . . . *minds* (Matthew 22:37). Paul's mode of operation in fulfilling his call to the Gentiles involved the use of logical thinking as he *reasoned daily* in the synagogues and in the school of Tyrannus concerning the identity of Jesus (Acts 17:2-3; 19:9-10).

It is the carnal mind that is against God, not the mind *per se*. The answer is not to reject the mind and rational thinking, but to renew the mind in God's Word as Paul admonishes in Romans 12:2. God's Word and Spirit will often transcend human reason, but they will never violate it or seek to eliminate it. Contemplative prayer devalues human words and thoughts in prayer and this is another reason I do not practice contemplative prayer.

Reason #3
The Goal of Contemplative Prayer is to Have a Mystical Encounter, Not to Know God and Develop an Obedient Relationship with Him.

My goal is not to have a spiritual experience or mystical encounter with God. My goal is to know Jesus Christ, have a personal relationship with Him, and be obedient to do His will. If I have a spiritual experience, so be it, but that is not my goal. My goal is to know Him and the starting point for knowing Him is the Scriptures.

For example, Luke 24:13-32 records the story of Jesus' post-resurrection appearance to two of His disciples as they walked the seven miles from Jerusalem to Emmaus. The two disciples did not recognize Jesus in His resurrected body as they shared with Him their sadness and disillusionment because the One they thought was the Messiah had just been crucified in Jerusalem.

Having just come out of the tomb by the greatest demonstration of power ever known, Jesus had many things He could have talked to them about. Instead, he spent the entire two hours going from Genesis to Malachi pointing out all the Scriptures that spoke of Himself.

Luke says, *And beginning with Moses and all the prophets, He expounded to them in all the Scriptures the things concerning Himself* (Luke 24:25-27).

It is significant that Jesus did not tell them of His incredible resurrection experience. Neither did He teach them some special prayer mantra or technique for encountering God. Instead, He spent this entire time making sure that they knew the Christ of Scripture.

For whatever reason, those who fall into the trap of pursuing spiritual experiences through contemplative prayer, tend to neglect the Scriptures. This was true in the medieval church as well as the contemporary church. Hans Kung, the most widely read Roman Catholic theologian in the world today, addressed this problem in Catholicism when he wrote,

> These new revelations not only overshadowed the Bible and the Gospel, but also Him whom the Gospel proclaims and to whom the Bible bears witness. It is striking how rarely Christ appeared in all these "revelations," "apparitions," and "wonders." Catholics who followed in the wake of every new "revelation," which often turned out to be fantasy or deceit, and indulged their desire for sensation by looking for the latest reports of miracles—and yet who had never once in their whole lives read the Scriptures from cover to cover.

Kung's evaluation of medieval Catholicism would, I suspect, fit many in Protestant charismatic circles today. Many run from conference to conference looking for where they can experience the biggest goose bumps or receive the latest and most exciting new revelation from Prophet so and so. Yet, when was the last time they prayerfully read through the Gospels and the New Testament?

I do not practice contemplative prayer because its very purpose and goal is contrary to Scripture and leads one away from a true knowledge of God and Christ.

Reason #4
Jesus Did not Teach Or
Practice Contemplative Prayer.

Jesus does not advocate any form of mystical prayer. He does not teach any postures or techniques for prayer and meditation. Neither is there any mention of silence or contemplation. Instead, He emphasizes a relational approach to God in which prayer is simple conversation with a loving, benevolent Being whom He calls *Abba*, an endearing term used only by children for the father in the Jewish household.

For Jesus, oneness with God is not a mystical union of one's being with God, but a practical oneness of will and purpose. *Not My will but Thine be done*, Jesus prayed, showing, that in His incarnate state, union with God consisted of a submission of His will to the will of the Father.

I cannot imagine Jesus and His disciples all sitting in the lotus position with their eyes closed seeking to go into a place of silence and contemplation where they will encounter God. Such a picture is completely contrary to what we know of Jesus from the Gospels. Jesus believed that God was continually with Him and He moved and acted in that confidence.

Another point of divergence of Jesus with mysticism is that He does not call His disciples to withdraw from the world into solitude and contemplation. Instead, He promises a baptism in the Holy Spirit that will empower His followers to prophetically engage the world as His witnesses.

I do not practice contemplative prayer because Jesus did not practice it, nor did He teach it to others.

Reason #5
The Early Church Did Not Teach
Or Practice Contemplative Prayer

The early church followed in the footsteps of Jesus and prayed dynamic, relational prayers in which they revered God's majesty and greatness, and asked for His help in the urgencies of their lives (see, for example, Acts 4:23-31). Although in their business of witnessing of Christ to their world they had what some would call mystical experiences (miracles, angelic deliverances, etc.), there is no evidence of them pursing spiritual experiences through silence and contemplation.

Although Paul had a supernatural encounter with the risen Lord on Damascus Road, he understood that this was a unique experience and he never used it to try and lead people into a similar encounter. Instead, he began with the Scriptures in his ministry of leading people to Christ. Luke says of Paul in Thessalonica that according to his custom, he *went in to them, and for three Sabbaths reasoned with them from the Scriptures* (Acts 17:3).

There are many recorded prayers in the New Testament. These prayers are all vocal, expressed to a God that they assume is personal and hears their spoken prayers.

I do not practice contemplative prayer because the early church did not practice it.

More in Common with Eastern Religions

Contemplative prayer, based in medieval mysticism, seems to have more in common with the mysticism of the East than it does with Biblical Christianity. This is why Kung writes,

> And yet we must realize that mysticism is not a specifically Christian phenomenon. Not only is mysticism older than Christianity; it also comes from far away. Mystical religion had already come into being at a very early stage – in the late Vedan period – in India.[24]

---

[24] Hans Kung, *Christianity: Essence, History, and Future* (New York: Continuum, 1995), 448.

Chapter 13

How to Test the Spirits

Beloved, do not believe every spirit, but test the spirits, whether they are of God; because many false prophets have gone out into the world.

I John 4:1

Scripture is clear that we are not to be passive concerning prophecy and claims of the supernatural. We are exhorted in the above verse to "test the spirits" and in I Corinthians 14:29 we are told to "judge" prophetic utterances. This then raises the question of how this is to be done? What are the criteria used to separate the true from the false?

In this chapter we will present five tests to be used in testing the spirits and judging prophetic utterances. These five tests include (1) a vision test, (2) a heart test, (3) a word test, (4) a freedom test and (5) a character test.

The Vision Test

This test is related to the focus, vision or goal of the person or message in question. What is their focus and preoccupation? What is their ultimate vision or goal? Is it themselves? Is it their own ministry? Or is it Jesus Christ?

In his introductory discussion of the gifts of the Spirit in I Corinthians 12:1-3, Paul makes it clear that gifts of the Spirit, including prophecy, must occur in a context where Jesus Christ is recognized and confessed as Lord, which is a confession of His deity and supremacy.

Commenting on this passage, Fee says;

> The ultimate criterion of the Spirit's activity is the exaltation of Jesus as Lord. Whatever takes away from that, even if they be legitimate expressions of the Spirit, begins to move away from Christ to a more pagan fascination with spiritual activity as an end in itself.[25]

When we examine the focus of the early church and the preaching of the apostles, we find that it is Christ. It is said of Philip in Acts 8:5 that he went down to Samaria *and peached Christ to them.* Acts 17:1-3 tells us how Paul, as his custom was, went into the synagogue and reasoned with them from the Scriptures explaining and demonstrating that, *This Jesus whom I preach to you is the Christ.* Paul's preaching was focused on Jesus!

It's interesting to note that in Acts every time there is a miracle, the miracle does not become the focus. They do not promote miracles or a miracle ministry. Instead, every miracle that occurs is taken as an opportunity to point people to Jesus. Jesus is the focal point. Jesus is the vision.

The Holy Spirit does not come to glorify angels, preachers, churches or denominations. In a recent "revival," the revivalist said that God told him, "People already know Jesus; they need to know the angel." That was not from God. The Holy Spirit will never, never displace Jesus with an angel

---

[25] Gordon Fee, *God's Empowering Presence,* 157-58.

The Holy Spirit is in the earth to lift up Jesus. Remember what the heavenly escort said to John when John, overwhelmed with the sights he was seeing, fell at his feet to worship him. This heavenly citizen immediately stopped him and said, *See that you do not do that!* He then said to John, *Worship God! For the testimony of Jesus is the spirit of prophecy.*

When faced with questionable situations, apply the vision test. Ask yourself about the person's vision. Do they have a vision to honor and glorify the Lord Jesus Christ? Or is their vision more about themselves? If their message is tinged with human pride and ego, then there is reason to "separate" this person and their message from your life. Remember the words of Jesus in John 16:14 where He said that when the Spirit of truth has come, *He will glorify Me.* It's all about Jesus! This is the Vision Test.

The Heart Test

I often receive emails from people telling about a meeting they attended, and although it was Christian, they will say that "something inside just didn't seem right." I always tell them, "Listen to your spirit! Listen to your heart!" The Holy Spirit—the Spirit of truth--who is on the inside of you will alert you and witness to truth.

Sometimes, however, what we are hearing and seeing may seem so impressive, and everyone around is so excited that we may tend to question ourselves and may end up telling ourselves we must be wrong, when we were actually right all along. Remember, if we are a committed follower of Jesus and truth, we can trust our heart.

John speaks of this heart test in I John 2:18-27. In verse 26 he makes clear that he is writing *concerning those who try to deceive you*. In other words, discriminating between that which is true and that which is false is the context in which John is writing. In 2:27 John then says;

> But the anointing which you have received from Him abides in you, and you do not need that anyone teach you; but as the same anointing teaches you concerning all things, and is true, and is not a lie, and just as it has taught you, you will abide in Him.

I have heard people interpret this passage to mean that they did not need to learn from any person for the Holy Spirit would directly teach them everything they needed to know. If that were the case, however, there would be no need for "teachers" in the church. This passage is directly related to discerning between the true and the false and John is saying that there is an "anointing" that every believer has received that will enable them to distinguish between what is true and what is false.

The Greek word for "anointing" in this passage is *chrisma* and is very similar to the Greek word for "Spiritual gift" in I Corinthians 12:4, which is *charisma*. Only the Greek letter *alpha* is missing from the word in I John.

I mention this to make the point that this "anointing" in I John 2:27 is something possessed by every true believer and is directly related to the indwelling presence of the Holy Spirit. Jesus, in John 16:13 promised that with the coming of the Holy Spirit, *He will guide you into all truth.* The Holy Spirit dwells on the inside, in the very core of our being and this is the place from which he will guide.

When facing questionable spiritual words or activity, remember that you have a truth detector on the inside of you. Listen to your heart. Do you have a sense of peace inside? Or is there a troubling or upset in your spirit? This is the Heart Test.

The Word Test

The Word Test asks, "Is it compatible with the overall testimony of God's word?" The Spirit and the Word agree. God will never say something today that contradicts, or is out of character, with what He has said in the past through the Scriptures. For example, God would never tell a man to divorce his wife and marry another woman, for that would contradict everything He has already said about marriage.

In Psalm 119:105 David said, *Your word is a lamp to my feet and a light to my path.* In II Timothy 3:16 Paul said, *All Scripture is given by inspiration of God and is profitable for doctrine, for reproof, for correction, for instruction in righteousness, that the person may be complete, lacking nothing.*

At the Azusa Street Revival (1906-09) where many spiritual manifestations were occurring, the leaders, including William Seymour, emphasized making the Bible the standard for judging those manifestations. In response to a question concerning whether it was necessary to study the Bible after being filled with the Holy Spirit, they answered;

Yes, if not we become fanatical or many times will be led by deceptive spirits and begin to have revelations and dreams contrary to the Word and begin to prophesy and think ourselves some great one, bigger than some other Christians. But by reading the Bible prayerfully, waiting before God, we become just humble little children, and we never feel that we have got more than the least of God's children.

The twenty-seven-books of the New Testament comprise what is called the New Testament "canon." The reason it is called "the canon" is that in ancient times a "canon" was a measuring tool, just as we have a measuring tape or a yard-stick. It was a reed or stiff piece of cane, or grass, that was used as a standard of measure.

Very early on the twenty-seven books of the New Testament were recognized as the canon, *i.e.,* the rule or standard, by which every other teaching, revelation and doctrine must be measured. Paul alludes to this in II Timothy 3:16-17 where he says,

All Scripture *is given by inspiration of God and is profitable for doctrine, for reproof, for correction, for instruction in righteousness that the servant of God may be complete, thoroughly equipped for every good work* (NIV).

When facing unusual spiritual issues and manifestations, bring the word of God to bear on the situation. As it says in Isaiah 8:20, *To the Law and to the testimony. If they do not speak according to this Word, it is because there is no light in them.*

The Freedom Test

In Galatians 5:1, Paul exhorts the Galatian believers to *stand fast in the freedom* they had experienced in Christ. There were Judaizers out of Jerusalem who had visited Galatia and told the new Gentile believers that their faith in Christ was not enough. According to the Judaizes, the men must be circumcised and they all must commit themselves to keep both the oral and written Jewish law, including the Sabbaths, festivals and multitude of regulations.

Jesus, however, had already addressed this matter in Matthew 11:28, where he said, *Come unto me all ye that labor and are heavy laden, and I will rest you* (literal translation). When I was young I thought Jesus, in this passage, was calling out to people burdened down with sins. I later learned that He was speaking to religious people who were burdened down with religious duty and obligation, which had been substituted for a living relationship with God.

The rabbis had identified 613 commands in the Torah; 365 prohibitions and 248 positive commands. The Pharisees of Jesus day believed that if all Israel kept all 613 commandments for one day then Messiah would come. They, therefore, called upon Jews to take upon themselves the "yoke of the law, by committing themselves to do their level best to keep all 613 commands. This had resulted in many in Israel being burdened down with heavy, religious duty. Jesus called them away from all this religion into a living relationship with Himself. (See Matt. 11:28-30)

This is what Paul is addressing in his letter to the Galatians. They are not to come under bondage to a religious system. They are to live holy lives out of a personal, living relationship with God through Jesus Christ.

Beware of any teaching or prophecy that would put you in obligation or bondage to a person, church or creed. Stand fast in the liberty of a living relationship with God through Jesus Christ.

This is Paul's concern for the Galatian believers who are being tempted to embrace religious legalism. This is why he admonishes,

> Stand fast therefore in the liberty by which Christ has made us free, and do not be entangled again with a yoke of bondage (Galatians 5:1).

The Character Test

One day, as a young believer, I passed a small church I had visited in the past and noticed a large banner in the yard with the name of a preacher and the caption in bold lettering, "God's 20th Century Prophet." That caught my attention and I could hardly wait to go and hear what this 20th century prophet had to say.

I attended the service that night and this individual preached but spent most of his time prophesying to people. He would walk down the aisle and pick people out of the congregation and prophesy to them. His prophecies were not practical but filled with images and symbolisms. Most people there seemed to be in awe of what they were hearing.

The meeting with "God's 20th Century Prophet" came to a sudden end when the pastor discovered, that in private, he had prophesied to members of the congregation to give him money, and even land.

If God did use him in a prophetic gift (and that is open to question), he had prostituted it for monetary gain. He fit the category of those whom Jude lamented; *Woe to them! For they have gone in the way of Cain, have run greedily in the error of Balaam for profit.* He failed the Character Test.

In Matthew 7:15 Jesus said, *Beware of false prophets, who come to you in sheep's clothing, but inwardly they are ravenous wolves.* The word "ravenous," that Jesus used to describe these false prophets, is an extreme form of greediness that will destroy others to get what it wants.

Jesus describes these false prophets as "ravenous wolves" dressed in "sheep's clothing." They've got all the right words; they know how to quote Scripture; they know how to prophesy with words that tickle the ears; but they are not what they appear to be. They have no integrity.

Jesus went on to say in vs. 16, *You will know them by their fruits.* Fruit relates to two things: (1) the character of the person, and (2) the fruit they produce in the lives of those who hear them.

A Christmas tree, for example, has all kinds of tinsel and bells on it, but those things do not tell you what kind of tree it is. In a similar way, a person may be a talented singer and a gifted orator with a charismatic personality, but that is tinsel and bells. It says nothing about their character.

To determine the kind of tree it is, you must find some fruit, *i.e.,* that which the tree has produced. If you pull aside the tinsel and bells and find a pine cone, then you know it is a pine tree. Jesus said, *You will know them by their fruits.*

Some will protest by saying, "Oh, we shouldn't judge anyone." When Jesus said, *Judge not lest you be judged*, he was talking about having a critical, censorious attitude, not about protecting ourselves from those who would harm us. The fact that He tells us in this passage to "beware" of false prophets involves a level of judgment by which we determine by their fruit that they are not legitimate. He is telling us to "think critically."

Paul also tells believers to make judgments concerning those who call themselves Christians but are immoral and ungodly. In fact, he instructs the Corinthian believers not to have fellowship with such people. In I Corinthians 5:11 he writes;

> *But now I have written to you not to keep company with anyone named a brother, who is sexually immoral, or covetous, or an idolater, or a reviler, or a drunkard, or an extortioner — not even to eat with such a person . . . therefore put away from yourselves the evil person.*

What we are talking about here is "testing the spirits," *i.e.,* doing what Scripture instructs us to do, for our own good and safety. Jesus, Paul and other New Testament writers admonish us to look at the fruit or character of a person's life and ministry in determining their legitimacy. This is the Character Test.

Concluding Thought

We are living in incredible times. We are living in the days when God said He would pour out His Spirit on all flesh. We are living at a time when the Gospel is being preached to every ethnicity as Jesus promised in Matthew 24:14.

We are also living in days of great deception, as Jesus and the New Testament writers warned. We must, therefore, be diligent to carry out the admonitions of Scripture to test the spirits whether they are of God, remembering that many deceivers and false prophets are in the world today.

Chapter 14

Believe in Miracles
But Follow Jesus

*If there arises among you a prophet or a dreamer of dreams, and he gives
you a sign or a wonder . . . saying, "Let us go after other gods"—which
you have not known—"and let us serve them," you shall not listen to the
words of that prophet or dreamer of dreams, for the Lord your God is
testing you to know whether you love the Lord your God with all your heart
and with all your soul.*

Deuteronomy 13:1-2

During a class I was teaching about revival and miracles,
a young man shared about being in a meeting where
miracles were being greatly publicized. He said that at
one point the crowd began to chant over and over,
"Signs! Miracles! Signs! Miracles!"

Choking back the tears, he said, "I felt grieved in my
spirit." He was also confused. Why did he feel grieved
inside? Aren't we supposed to desire miracles? I assured
him that what he experienced was the Holy Spirit in him
being grieved by this crowd's unhealthy preoccupation
and fascination with miracles. Jesus had been preempted
by their self-centered desire to see a miracle.

This reminded me of Herod who was "exceedingly glad"
to finally see Jesus when Pilate sent Jesus to him during
His trial. Why was Herod "exceedingly glad" to see
Jesus? It wasn't because Herod wanted to know Him and
His message. Luke 23:8 says, "He hoped to see some
miracle done by Him." Herod wanted to be entertained

by a miracle. His interest in Jesus and miracles was centered in himself and his own egotistical desire.

Believers are not to follow signs; signs are to follow believers. Mk. 16:15 says, *These signs shall follow (accompany) them that believe.* Believers are to follow Jesus and let the signs follow where they will. The devil can perform signs and if we are following signs, we are headed for trouble. Here are some suggestions to help keep us on track:

1) Remember that Jesus is the source of true and genuine miracles, so seek Him.
2) Remember that a miracle is not an end in itself, to be sought for its own value. Its only value is in bringing glory to Jesus and helping someone in need.
3) Remember that the primary purpose of miracles is to honor and exalt the name of Jesus, not build up a preacher, church or ministry.
4) Don't follow signs. Follow Jesus and let the signs follow you.
5) Beware of those who would nurture an unhealthy fascination with miracles instead of a closer, more intimate walk with Jesus.
6) Avoid the Herod mentality that wants to be entertained by a miracle in much the same way that people pay to be entertained by a magician.
7) Believe in miracles, but follow Jesus

T.L. Osborn Expresses Concern

The above chapter was first published as an article in 2005. The late, Dr. T.L. Osborn, who was the father of modern, miracle evangelism, read the article and sent the following email.

Hello Brother Eddie:

Congratulations on your newsletter: "Believe in Miracles But Follow Jesus." We are facing a real serious plague of superstition in the body of the Pentecostal and charismatic world. I am often embarrassed, shocked, ashamed, by the silly things people are doing and saying. Keep up the good work. We must let the world know that somebody, somewhere is being faithful to Gospel Redemption teaching.

Greetings to you both. You are special. The writings that both of you are offering to our world are of tremendous spiritual value.

Your special friend and co-worker with Christ,

T.L. Osborn

Selected Bibliography

David Aune, *Prophecy in Early Christianity and the Ancient Mediterranean World.* Grand Rapids: Eerdmans, 1983.

Finney, Charles G. *An Autobiography.* Old Tappan, NJ: Fleming H. Revell, 1908.

___. *Revival Lectures.* Grand Rapids: Fleming H. Revell, n.d.

Hyatt, Eddie. *2000 Years of Charismatic Christianity.* Lake Mary, FL, 2002.

___. *Revival Fire: Discerning Between the True & the False.* Grapevine, TX: Hyatt Press, 2008.

Hyatt, Susan. *In the Spirit We're Equal.* Dallas: Hyatt Press, 1998.

Kung, Hans. *The Church.* Garden City, NY: Image Books, 1976.

___. *Christianity: Essence, History, and Future.* New York: Continuum, 1995.

Strickland, W.P., Ed., *Autobiography of Peter Cartwright, The Backwoods Preacher.* New York: Carlton & Porter, 1857.

Torrey, R. A. *The Power of Prayer and the Prayer of Power.* Grand Rapids: Zondervan, 1924.

Tucker, Ruth. *Another Gospel.* Grand Rapids: Zondervan, 2004.

Whitefield, George. *George Whitefield's Journals.* Carlisle, PA: Banner of Truth Trust, 1960.

Wesley, John. *The Works of John Wesley.* 14 Vols. Grand Rapids: Zondervan, n.d.

About the Author

 Dr. Eddie L. Hyatt is a seasoned minister of the Gospel with over 45 years of ministerial experience as a pastor, Bible teacher and Professor of Theology. He holds the Doctor of Ministry from Regent University as well as the Master of Divinity and a Master of Arts from Oral Roberts University. He has authored several books, including *2000 Years of Charismatic Christianity*, which is used as a textbook in colleges and seminaries around the world. Eddie resides in Grapevine, TX with his wife, Dr. Susan Hyatt, from where he carries on a ministry of writing, teaching and preaching. To schedule him to speak in your church, group or conference, send an email to dreddiehyatt@gmail.com. And visit his website at www.eddiehyatt.com.

Eddie is also working with his wife, Dr. Susan Hyatt, in establishing the Int'l Christian Women's Hall of Fame and Ministry Center on Main Street in Grapevine, Texas. To learn more about how you can be involved, email drsuehyatt@.live.com and visit the website at https://www.gwtwchristianwomenshalloffame.com.

For discounts on bulk orders of this book,
send an email to dreddiehyatt@gmail.com.

Other Books by Drs. Eddie & Susan Hyatt

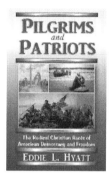 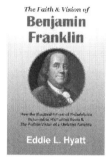 

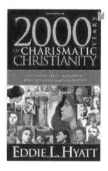 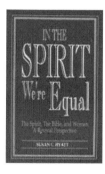 

These and other materials are available from Amazon
and from www.eddiehyatt.com and
www.godswordtowomen.org.

Made in the USA
Coppell, TX
21 May 2021

56089376R00074